11/7/95

MODERN SCHOLARSHIP ON
EUROPEAN HISTORY

Henry A. Turner, Jr.
General Editor

In 1948, after the holocaust of World War
II, a military alliance known as the Western
European Union was formed by Britain,
France, and the Benelux countries. The following year they joined with five other European powers, the United States, and Canada
in forming the North Atlantic Treaty Organization (NATO). That same year the
Council of Europe was created at Strasbourg
by ten non-Communist countries. But none
of these constituted integration because none
was given supranational powers.

Disgust with the cautious attitude of the
British and Scandinavian members of the
Council of Europe drove the "Six" (France,
West Germany, Italy, Belgium, the Netherlands, and Luxembourg) to form their first
supranational union, the European Coal and
Steel Community, in 1950. In 1957 they then
created not only the European Atomic Energy Community (Euratom), which was a
disappointment from the start, but finally
the European Economic Community (EEC),
or Common Market. In 1972 the United
Kingdom, Ireland, and Denmark joined the
Common Market, increasing its membership to nine.

Professor Willis has selected articles that
examine this movement toward European
integration from the viewpoint of historian,
economist, and political scientist. Their usefulness here lies in part in their contribution
to the answering of the crucial question:
Has integration advanced to the point where
its achievements are irreversible—or at least
reversible only at prohibitive cost?

EUROPEAN INTEGRATION

EUROPEAN INTEGRATION

EDITED WITH AN INTRODUCTION BY F. ROY WILLIS

NEW VIEWPOINTS
A Division of Franklin Watts, Inc.   New York 1975

EUROPEAN INTEGRATION

Copyright © 1975 by F. Roy Willis
All rights reserved, including the right to reproduce
this book or portions thereof in any form

Library of Congress Cataloging in Publication Data
Main entry under title:

European Integration.

    (Modern scholarship on European history)
    Bibliography: p.
    Includes index.
    1. Europe — Economic integration — History — Ad-
dresses, essays, lectures. 2. European federation. I. Willis,
Frank Roy.
HC241.2.E858   330.9′4′055   75-8842
ISBN 0-531-05371-7
ISBN 0-531-05578-7 pbk.

Manufactured in the United States of America
6 5 4 3 2 1

CONTENTS

INTRODUCTION ix

**1
EUROPEAN FEDERATION IN THE POLITICAL
THOUGHT OF RESISTANCE MOVEMENTS
DURING WORLD WAR II** 1
BY WALTER LIPGENS

**2
SCHUMAN BREAKS THE DEADLOCK** 19
BY F. ROY WILLIS

**3
THE DEFEAT OF THE EUROPEAN ARMY** 38
BY HENRI BRUGMANS

**4
POSITIVE INTEGRATION AND NEGATIVE
INTEGRATION: SOME PROBLEMS OF
ECONOMIC UNION IN THE EEC** 50
BY JOHN PINDER

CONTENTS

**5
THEORETICAL APPROACHES TO
EUROPEAN INTEGRATION**   84
BY MARIE-ELISABETH DE BUSSY, HÉLÈNE DELORME,
AND FRANÇOISE DE LA SERRE

**6
THE EUROPEAN ECONOMIC COMMUNITY
AND THE 1965 CRISIS**   130
BY FRANÇOISE DE LA SERRE

**7
THE UTILITY OF THE EEC EXPERIENCE
FOR EASTERN EUROPE**   154
BY WERNER FELD

BIBLIOGRAPHY   189

INDEX   195

INTRODUCTION

By European integration, we mean the process of political and economic unification of the nation-states of Europe, and primarily of those of Western Europe, in the period since the end of the Second World War in 1945. "Integration" is distinguished from "cooperation" by the fact that participants in integration must delegate a portion of their national sovereignty to a body with supranational powers.

The origins of the movement have been sought in the fairly distant past. Italians like to find them in the Roman Empire and the Catholic Church. Both Germans and Frenchmen have suggested that Charlemagne was the precursor of a united Europe. But the first political theorists to condemn the nation-state as it had developed in Europe at the end of the Middle Ages and to propose European union as a solution were the Duc de Sully in the early seventeenth century and the Abbé de Saint-Pierre a century later. Sully proposed a "Most Christian Council," begun— perhaps because he was a French Protestant—by the Germans; and he even suggested that peace be kept by a European army. Saint-Pierre suggested that the sovereigns of Europe should delegate part of their sovereignty to a European senate, support it financially, and provide military force in its defense. The nineteenth century sanctified the principle of nationalism; and most of its rebellions, suppressed or successful, and the majority of its wars, were due to the desire of national groups to form their own nation-states or of other states to prevent them from doing so. Even so, many political theorists looked to the day when the nation-states would join together in some superior federation. Giuseppe Mazzini, for example, not only looked to the formation of a republican nation-state of Italy but to its submersion in the "moral unity of Europe." Yet these views have only academic interest; no one took their proponents seriously. Even after the carnage of the First World War, which could hardly have been surpassed as a demonstration of the inadequacy of a state system composed of competing nation-states, cynical Old World statesmen regarded such proposals as French Foreign Minister Aristide Briand's Memorandum of 1930 in favor of a "United States of Europe" as ingenuous posturing. It was left to Adolf Hitler to declare with more substance that he was the genuine uniter of Europe. Scholars have therefore given justifiably little thought to the origins of the integration movement, except to seek the source of the "idea" of Europe and the possible roots of a sense of European consciousness.

The European federalist movement, which in the first postwar decade was the vanguard of the campaign for European unification, developed with enormous speed during the Resistance movements, as Walter Lipgens demonstrates in his contribution to this volume. Italian federalists like Ernesto Rossi and Altiero Spinelli concerted their ideas on the prison-island of Ventotene. German federalists like Eugen Kogon met similar-minded leaders in the Nazi concentration camps. During the war, at great personal risk, underground leaders from all over Europe met to draw up manifestoes and more concrete schemes for the federal union they hoped would replace the discredited nation-states when the fighting stopped. Their first, and greatest, disappointment was to find themselves ignored when the occupying armies, in both Eastern and Western Europe, handed over political controls to restored national governments. The communization of Eastern Europe in 1944–48, carried out piece-meal in each separate nation-state, imposed impossible barriers to the formation of an all-European union; and only later, under the influence of the successful economic integration in Western Europe, did the East European states themselves undertake through Comecon (Council for Mutual Economic Assistance) to harmonize their economic planning, as is revealed in the final chapter of this volume.

The Cold War was thus the context in which the European integration movement was re-born; and it was the failure to recover economically, in what was generally regarded as imminent danger of Communist attack from without or subversion from within, that prompted the first faltering moves towards greater cooperation. To guard against the military threat from the Soviet Union, Britain joined with France and the Benelux countries in 1948 in the military alliance known as the Western European Union; and the following year the five joined with five other European powers, the United States, and Canada in forming the North Atlantic Treaty Organization (NATO). While these alliances implied greater military coordination than previously undertaken, they did not require the surrender of any portion of national sovereignty. (Little attempt has been made by scholars to set the European integration movement in its Cold War setting. The parameters of Cold War rivalry have been largely taken for granted, and fruitful "revisionist" work remains to be done.)

The much-heralded Council of Europe, created at Strasbourg in 1949 by ten non-Communist countries of Europe, was also given no supranational powers. It did much useful work. It accustomed European parliamentarians to regular debates in the Consultative Assembly on matters of common concern, especially regarding human rights, and it developed three transnational political parties (Christian Democrats, Socialists, and Liberals).

Nevertheless, disgust with the Council of Europe, or in reality with the cautious attitude of the British and Scandinavian members, drove the "Six" (France, West Germany, Italy, Belgium, the Netherlands, Luxembourg) to attempt to form the first supranational union, the European Coal and Steel Community.

From this point, the personal influence of Jean Monnet, head of the French Planning Commissariat in 1950, runs through the whole integration movement. In a perfectly timed coup, Monnet presented a plan for the integration of the coal and steel industries of Western Europe to the French Foreign Minister Robert Schuman on the morning of May 9, and persuaded him to push it through the cabinet the same day. Thus, in his famous press conference that afternoon, Schuman was able to announce that France was taking the first step toward formation of Europe's first supranational union, the European Coal and Steel Community, whose inception is analyzed in detail in this volume's second chapter. Monnet thus became the exponent of the so-called functional approach to European integration, the unification of individual sectors of the economy by nations agreeing to participate in a partial form of supranational union. Complete economic union would follow the success of a partial or sectoral union, Monnet felt, and this success would then lead to wider political union.

The federalist movements, however, were impatient with the patently technocratic character of the European Coal and Steel Community (ECSC) as it was shaped in the treaty negotiations of 1950–51. They welcomed the opportunity to harness American pressure for the rearmament of West Germany, which resulted from American involvement in the Korean war, to the formation of an integrated military community in Western Europe. The French Premier, René Pleven, proposed in October 1950 that the national armies of Western Europe, including forces from West Germany, should be merged in a European Defense Community (EDC), similar in organization to the European Coal and Steel Community. The federalists then argued that a European army could only be directed by a European government; and, on the proposal of Italian Premier Alcide De Gasperi and French Foreign Minister Schuman, an *ad hoc* assembly, formed by enlargement of the Common Assembly of ECSC, was directed to draw up a political statute for a European Political Community (EPC). The long, troubled history of the negotiation of the EDC Treaty and its eventual defeat in the French parliament on August 30, 1954, is related by Henri Brugmans, one of Europe's leading federalists, in his contribution to this volume. The collapse of these hopes of dramatic advance toward military and political union marked the end of the idealistic, federalist phase of the European integration movement. For better or worse, impetus could be revived only by concentration on the economic, and many would argue the technocratic, aspect of integration.

In the aftermath of the defeat of EDC, both right-wing and extreme left-wing forces demanded the abandonment of the European Coal and Steel Community itself; but the seizure of the initiative, for a brief but crucial period, by the governments of Belgium and the Netherlands revived the drive toward economic union. At Messina, Sicily, in June 1955, the foreign ministers of the Six accepted the far-sighted Belgian and Dutch proposals for preliminary study of a European Economic Community (EEC), or Common Market, and a European Atomic Energy Community (Euratom). In the two years of negotiations that culminated in the signing of the Treaties of Rome in March 1957, instituting a European Economic Community and a European Atomic Energy Community, European statesmen faced enormous technical problems in creating a customs union that could eventually evolve into a full-fledged economic union and finally into a political union. Economic theory on the nature and effects of customs unions was still in its infancy at that time, the pioneering study being Jacob Viner's *The Customs Union Issue*, published in 1950; and as a result, much of the debate over the ratification of the treaties was concerned with the possible economic sacrifices the six future members of EEC were being called upon to make for a common political benefit. These economic issues are succinctly presented in the study in this volume by John Pinder, who emphasizes the political implications of seemingly technical economic decisions.

Euratom was a disappointment from the start, since its members continued to press on with their own national atomic energy programs and gave only minor projects and financing to the new Community. Little scholarly work has therefore been devoted to it. The European Economic Community, however, proved a far greater economic success than had been hoped. The industrial customs union was achieved with little difficulty. By 1961 import quotas among member states had been abolished. In 1968 tariffs on both industrial and agricultural goods traded among member states had been removed. Free movement of labor within the Community had been facilitated by preferential treatment to Community nationals as against immigrants from outside the Community. Moreover, the return of General de Gaulle to power in France in June 1958 had strengthened the Community in many ways. De Gaulle, although insistent upon the European vocation of the Community as a call to independence from the United States and on the nation-state as the fundamental building-block of the union, had forced his partners to acceptance of Community-wide policies of special interest to France by threat of a French veto. Without de Gaulle's insistence, it is doubtful whether the Community could have worked out a common agricultural policy at all. However, in the "empty chair" crisis of 1965-66, de Gaulle came close to destroying the Community itself.

No crisis better illustrates the difficulty of seeking to use economic integration as a prelude to political integration, and none throws more light upon the impact of Gaullist policies on the evolution of the Common Market. The chapter in this volume by the French political scientist Françoise de la Serre indicates how the French government was able to make use of the Community's political machinery to advance its own national interests in the formulation of common policies within EEC, and thus to some extent to engage in "power politics" within a Community whose purpose was to reduce the scope of such national self-assertion. At the same time, however, the crisis must be related to a broader interpretation of Community goals. Was de Gaulle correct in asserting that the federalist notion of the emergence of a common European consciousness or even nationalism was unrealistic and that the way to concrete progress within EEC was by recognizing the value of the constituent nationalisms?

The interest of political scientists in European integration has centered on this question of how a politically integrated community comes into being. Historians, as the first three chapters of this book reveal, have tended to concentrate on the political decision-making by which the powers of the nation-state would be surrendered and on the pressure groups within the nations demanding such a surrender. The economist has been concerned with the material gains or losses of production, in the first place from product market integration and in the second place from the establishment of common economic policies. A whole new field of theoretical political science has, however, been created to deal with the problems of regional political integration. Although most of these theorists are American, they have found in the development of Europe's supranational communities a major source of their subject matter. This vast body of work is epitomized in the fifth chapter of this volume, "Theoretical Approaches to European Integration," by Marie-Elisabeth de Bussy, Hélène Delorme, and Françoise de la Serre. It will introduce the non-specialist to the main tools of analysis that have been developed over the past two decades by the two schools of "transactionalists" and "neofunctionalists." For the transactionalists, of whom Karl Deutsch is the leading theorist, European integration is interesting as an example of the increase of the intensity of communications and thus of a sense of community that transcends the pre-existing relationships within the nation-state. The emphasis is placed upon the correlation of transaction flows, such as trade and tourism, with the changing attitudes of both elite and mass groups. For the neofunctionalists, of whom Ernst Haas is the most significant, the most important feature of European integration is the shift of "loyalties, expectations and political activities" toward the Community authorities. Haas in particular emphasized the possibility of "spill-over," i.e., that experience in sectoral integration like ECSC might lead individuals participating in the process of sectoral integration to apply the methods of integration in wider areas. American political scientists have therefore devoted much research to establishing whether shifts of loyalties among elite groups participating in the work of the European Coal and Steel Community or the Common Market were in fact occurring, and whether membership in the European Communities exerted any significant influence upon public opinion concerning political integration.

After a decade of activity, the economic success of the European Economic Community seemed assured; but political integration within the Community had made little progress. Public opinion, in the atmosphere of détente between the United States and Russia, had lost interest in the federalist goals and had come to regard the Community authorities in Brussels as yet another faceless bureaucracy. As early as 1958 transactionalist theorists such as Deutsch had predicted a stagnation. To restore momentum, the Community members embarked upon several far-reaching programs, whose success is still uncertain. After long, complex negotiations, the Community was broadened in 1972 by the admission of the United Kingdom, Ireland, and Denmark. At the summit conference in October 1972 a number of ambitious new programs were approved, including the institution of a Community regional fund for aid to the lesser developed areas of EEC. And the completion of full economic union by 1980 was called for. Within two years many of these hopes were shattered. When the Arab states cut back their oil supplies to Western Europe and completely banned supplies for the Netherlands, following the Arab-Israeli war in 1973, the EEC members sought individual concessions from the Arab powers and conspicuously failed to share their fuel supplies with the Dutch. The second summit conference at Copenhagen in December 1973 made no concrete achievements, the heads of state and government merely agreeing to speed up planning for economic and monetary union. In 1974 the newly elected Labour government in Britain announced its determination to withdraw from the Community unless successful in renegotiating the terms of British entry.

Thus, almost thirty years after the end of the Second World War, which had appeared to most Europeans as irrefutable proof of the need for reducing the capacity for internecine struggles of the European nation-states, the progress of integration was gravely threatened. The usefulness of the articles collected in this book lies in part in their contribution to the answering of the crucial question: Has European integration advanced to the point where its achievements are irreversible, or at least reversible only at prohibitive cost?

EUROPEAN FEDERATION IN THE POLITICAL THOUGHT OF RESISTANCE MOVEMENTS DURING WORLD WAR II
BY WALTER LIPGENS

European federalism first became an important political force in the Resistance movements in states under Nazi or Fascist occupation. Both the idealism and the specific ideas for political and economic union, as the German historian Walter Lipgens demonstrates, were the reaction of deeply dedicated leaders to a war they felt had been made possible only by the division of Europe into nation-states. This chapter originally appeared as an article in Central European History, *Vol. I (1), March 1968, pp. 5–19. Copyright © 1968 by Emory University. It is reprinted by permission of the journal and the author.*

The experiences and catastrophes of the Second World War fundamentally affected European political attitudes.[1] Particularly intensive was the reconsideration of fundamental problems that went on in the non-communist resistance groups in the Nazi-occupied countries of Europe. What were their political plans? Research on the resistance movements is still in its early stages; however, there is already general agreement that the resistance movements did not fight for a return to prewar conditions, but for a new European society.[2] In particular, as several writers have pointed out, the goal of a democratic federation of all European nations appears repeatedly in the newspapers and proclamations of the Resistance.[3] To describe the ideas of the Resistance on European federation requires a thorough study of the documentary material on the various European resistance movements, with particular attention to those texts concerned with the future relationships of the European states; the following pages are a first report of the findings of such a study.[4]

But it is already difficult, more than twenty years after the end of the war, for us to understand the political attitudes of the resistance movements, which were developed in contexts and circumstances so very different from our own. We must therefore begin with a look at the conditions under which the thought of the Resistance developed, before turning to the Resistance writings themselves as they relate to a new organization of Europe. Finally, we may ask why the hopes and plans of the Resistance for a united Europe were not realized when the Hitler regime collapsed.

I

The first prerequisite for an understanding of the writings of the Resistance is to keep in mind the collapse of the European national states during the Second World War. Indeed it was the prime fact of this war—in contrast to the First World War—that (with the exception of Great Britain and four small nations, which Hitler permitted to remain neutral) all states on the European continent collapsed under Hitler's attack. Regimes of different social and political character were overwhelmed by the Germans, and thus demonstrated that they were no longer able to guarantee their people that minimum of security and independence that is the basic reason for their existence. Willingly or reluctantly they accepted the status of provinces or satellites in Hitler's empire, and placed their governing apparatus in its service. The historical significance and the effect of this violent lesson on the people of continental Europe can hardly be overestimated. The successive collapse of the states made people realize that the old forms were no longer militarily and politically viable. Even more important than the collapse itself is the fact that most people obviously felt this fate was deserved. Their experiences under the idea of the national state between 1919 and 1939 had been too painful and too disappointing. The sufferings of the First World War had produced a great longing for peace; but this desire had not been fulfilled by the national governments. Twenty years of uneasy peace had ended in an even more disastrous war. Nor had the European governments been able to deal with the constant economic crises, and this had already led a good many people to suspect that their states were too small to manage their economic affairs. No one wanted to return to such conditions. But not only the states had shown themselves to be inadequate: the structures of society itself were disintegrating. Authors of the Resistance were to write a great deal about "the tendency of anarchic dissolution" in the "collapse of personal security and social life throughout Europe." It is not necessary to go into details here. If we recognize that the Resistance leaders felt they were living at the end of an epoch in Europe, in a period of deepest cultural crisis, then we have taken the first essential step toward an understanding of their political plans.

A second factor that must be kept in mind is the manner in which totalitarianism imposed itself on this chaos. Throughout Europe, between the wars, fascist groups had emerged with their message that strength, ruthlessness, and discipline would cure the ills of society and the state. The Nazis were only the most successful among many. After 1939 the majority of the population in each country that was occupied by the Germans at first showed itself willing to collaborate with the victors and work with them to create a new Europe. But soon they had to realize that the Nazi leaders were not prepared to enter into any true cooperation; they could think only in terms of a primitive national imperialism and of colonial subjection of the nations. The degree of compulsion they were prepared to employ meant that the majority of peoples everywhere simply obeyed them—they did not enter the Resistance. The collapse of the social and ethical structures that had commenced long before now contributed to the penetration and control of totalitarian rule.

The third prerequisite for a proper evaluation of the Resistance texts is an understanding of the nature of the Resistance movements. There continues to be a widespread belief that these movements were semi-military in character, that they were largely occupied with sabotage, terror, assassination. But this conception is quite inaccurate. Between 1939 and 1944, as long as the totalitarian police and control apparatus remained effective, terror actions were almost impossible. A group that attempted them committed suicide. Behind the Russian front and in the Balkans conditions were different, but in Central and Western Europe even the larger resistance organizations could not think of undertaking serious military actions until Nazi control began to weaken in 1944. Military action was intensified by the communists in the last months of the war. But until then—that is to say, for the duration of the Nazi rule—the true character of the resistance movements was that of an intellectual resistance. It is this intellectual opposition that constitutes the most important achievement of the Resistance in Italy and Germany as well as in the occupied countries. The main activities of all resistance groups between 1940 and 1944 consisted of two things: of sheltering persecuted people, and of printing underground literature that accused the Nazi regime and appealed to faith and humanity as the true principles and guides to a better future. In general the movements were composed of small intellectual elites, scattered through the towns and cities, with little knowledge of each other's existence. To be sure, a considerable portion of the population in all countries, especially the still consciously Christian segments, became increasingly hostile toward the Nazi regime and its non-German servants. A sense of the genuine and enduring

European tradition awakened as people became aware of the totalitarian character of the Nazi system, of its methods and of its goals. Men again began to long for freedom and justice. Mussolini's political prisons and those of the collaborationist regimes were filled to capacity; and over a million Germans were thrown into concentration camps for their political attitudes. But most of those were people who had been caught reading or quoting illegal printed matter; the members of the resistance groups who wrote these texts were not numerous.

From the foregoing, the character, the significance, and the importance of the Resistance writings can be seen. They were not marginal efforts, produced in addition to military actions by a few intellectuals. On the contrary, for years, during which other forms of opposition were hardly possible, these writings *were* the Resistance. The most important function of the movements could only be to formulate ethical and political principles that would help people to live through the totalitarian experience and that would strengthen their opposition to it. Most groups began their existence in order to publish and distribute illegal newspapers or leaflets. Their leaders were also the editors-in-chief of these publications. In their leading articles they sought to define the possibilities for intellectual and spiritual resistance, to counteract tendencies to passive surrender to the totalitarian state, to mobilize intellectual opposition, to point to a better future.

The main purpose of these writings was to appeal for opposition to the totalitarian state, but not for a return to the conditions of the past, which had favored the development of totalitarian ideas. A sense of fellowship transcending national frontiers was felt by the members of the Resistance. In the words of a French writer: "We are united from the North Pole to the Pyrenees, from the English Channel to the Aegean Sea, in the same struggle against the same enemy: the struggle for freedom against slavery, justice against injustice, law against force."[5] Their consciousness of being members of a European crusade against National Socialism inspired Resistance authors again and again to similar statements. These principles were supported by specific plans for a better future. Heading almost every proposal were demands for the restitution of human rights against the claims of every kind of collectivism: "Down-trodden justice must be restored. . . . Freedom of belief and of conscience must be guaranteed . . . the inalienable worth of the human being is the basis of the law and order we are fighting for."[6] Likewise, proposals for future domestic policies were characterized by a determination to create a counterpoise to the state's claim to totality. These proposals contained demands for a thorough limiting of the state's authority, for the possibility of self-government in districts and regions, for regional federalism as opposed to the centralized national state. "Decentralization" and "self-government by the separate regions" were ever-recurring slogans. The following quotation characterized the feeling of all non-communist resistance groups: "Democratic principles of self-government are the only guarantees against the absolutist, centralizing power of the sovereign national state."[7]

In short, the resistance movements did not simply plead for a return to the old political forms. For all non-communist Resistance leaders, nationalism was the mark of the Nazis; resistance to the Nazis meant opposition to nationalism. As *Franc-tireur*, the organ of the socialist Resistance in southern France, put it: "Who would dare to impute to those masses who have risen in Europe against Nazi rule that they are fighting for the revival of a past whose profound weaknesses and irrevocable collapse they have experienced? Their goal is a new world!"[8]

II

Let us now try to get a clearer picture of those parts of the Resistance programs that concerned the future coexistence of the European peoples. Even a small sampling of the enormous quantity of material bearing upon this shows, in the first place, that the entire phenomenon of resistance was the result of a horrified rejection of the totalitarian state, of that "total control" by which the fascist doctrines had wished to assure a continuance of the sovereign national state in an altered environment. To the Resistance writers it became evident (in the words of an Italian document which has many parallels in all other countries) that in the hands of the old national states "the power to decide matters of war and peace, the power to control national armies, the power to divide the world into separate economic areas . . . the power to create despotism in a state, without outside interference," that all these components of power became "necessarily tools of destruction, of barbarism and suppression."[9] In the same sense, Heuven Goedhart, one of the leaders of the Resistance in Holland, defined "this war as the great crisis of the 'sovereignty of the state.' " The old extremes of power, according to Goedhart, had to be taken away from the national states and transferred to higher authorities.[10] In short, even in those parts of their programs that dealt with foreign affairs, the resistance movements opposed the claim of the state to totality. Instead they demanded a European federation within the framework of a world peace organization. Only in this way (according to the leader of *Défense de la France*) could "the main obstacle standing in the way of a free community be overcome: *the terrible inevitability of totalitarian rule as it is necessarily forged by nationalism.*"[11] The experience of the resistance movements under totalitarian rule explains the difference between their arguments and those of the men who in the twenties and thirties had demanded the unification of Europe for rational, geopolitical, or economic reasons. And for the same reason we note a difference in tone between the Resistance and people in exile. The writers of the Resistance denied all claims by the state to absolute power and were not satisfied with loose or symbolic associations or with only a few adaptations to economic and political expansion. The "policy of non-interference," the complement to the doctrine of sovereignty, in the words of a spokesman of the Italian *Resistenza*, "had destroyed European democracy."[12] And one of the Dutch writers stated: "Countries in which the most basic human rights are brutally violated become dangerous centers of infection, which the community of nations must have the right to oppose. The sanctity of state sovereignty has collapsed."[13]

From this central idea—namely the struggle against national sovereignty—and from the experiences with the League of Nations derived concern with the manner in which an effective European Federation should be constituted. Within the Resistance of each country there were smaller rightist groups—the O.C.M. in Paris, the Beck-Goerdeler Group in Berlin, etc.— which, to be sure, affirmed the necessity of binding international law and of an economic union, but which also wanted the states to retain a certain independence in foreign policy. They spoke of a "European Directorate" for the prevention of war and of a "European Economic Council," and for the most part came to the conclusion that, after all their experiences, these "councils" would have to have "police power" and the means to carry through their decisions. But they still tried to find a solution that would leave the states a certain freedom of decision, making Europe more a confederation than a federation.[14] However, the great majority of writers of the Resistance opposed any degree of state sovereignty in the areas of foreign policy, economics, and defense. This time, they said, the mistake of 1919, the weakness of the League of Nations, had to be avoided. The comparison with the League of Nations and investigation into the failure of this first attempt at international peace-keeping recur again and again in the writings of the Resistance of all countries. And these writings always came to the same conclusion: The League of Nations failed (in the words of a statement from the French Resistance) "because it was not one great autonomous power, independent of the national sovereignties and over them; because it possessed neither political authority nor material power for carrying out its decisions which would have been superior to those of the states."[15] As we read in a publication of the Italian Resistance, all mere leagues of states must fail, like the American Confederation of 1776, "because they possessed no decision-making body and no executive power of their own, but were dependent upon the unanimous vote of the associated states."[16] This comparison is often to be found in the writings of the Resistance. Just as the loosely united North American states in the Confederation of 1776 after thirteen difficult years recognized that peace and economy could not prosper in such a system and chose to form an effective federation in 1789, so too did the European states, after the failure of the League of Nations, have to make the decision to form an effective federation. This necessary step could not immediately be made on a global basis, since presumably the United States and the Soviet Union were not yet prepared to form a global federation. A common manifesto of representatives of the Resistance from nine European countries stated in 1944: "The lack of cultural unity which still persists in the various parts of the world does not permit an immediate creation of an organization that would bring together all cultures under a single federal government."[17] The "wearisome task" of global federation, one French writer asserts, "can not be undertaken with any prospect of success until a solution has first been found for Europe, the source of the catastrophes which have shaken the world time and again." It must be emphasized that the writings of the Resistance expressly rejected a "European nationalism," that they recommended the early independence of the colonies and pleaded for the inclusion of the European federation in a world peace organization. Only then could the European federation, as we read in many writings, "by its example urge the world to strive for a federative world organization."[18]

The formation of a powerful European Federal Government was in every country considered to be the absolutely essential first step forward. In the Polish underground the delegates of three of the four illegal parties prepared a common program of principles, in which the section on foreign policy read as follows: "The Polish Republic will be a member of the federation of free European nations. In this federation the Republic will work hard to further the greatest possible unity, and to support a Federal Government which must be powerful enough to protect the federated nations from external attack and to suppress all attempts to foster inner dissension through exaggerated nationalism."[19] The statement of principles upon which the Kreisau group (intellectually the most significant body of the German Resistance) based its planning began with the sentences: "Europe is a federal state possessing uniform sovereignty. . . . The federation is competent for foreign policy, defense and economy."[20] The most important Dutch Resistance publication, *Het Parool*, demanded that "a new super-government must be formed in Europe: a European federation which possesses the means to carry out its will and to impose it on the national sub-units."[21] The program of an Italian resistance group stated: "The maintenance of freedom and security on the entire Continent should be solely in the hands of the European federation and its executive, legislative, and judiciary organs."[22] Finally, the call of the Lyon region of the French Resistance provides a good summary: "The common federative state" must possess "the right to organize the economic life of Europe; the sole right to direct military forces and to move against any attempt to reconstruct a fascist regime; the right to regulate foreign relations; the right to administer those colonial territories which are not yet ready for independence. It must create a European citizenship in addition to the national one. The government of the federative state is not to be chosen by the national states, but by the people, in democratic and direct elections."[23] These statements in favor of a European federation —representative of hundreds of others—were in the last analysis based on one fundamental conviction: in the midst of a bitter struggle against an exaggerated nationalism none of the resistance groups could imagine that the European people would ever be able to return to the system of national states that had caused two terrible world wars.

III

The writers of the Resistance were convinced of the necessity of a European federation; the problem was its implementation.

At a conference in Switzerland in May 1944 the representatives of resistance groups of nine countries met and again urged that the Allied nations, which alone could defeat Hitler, "should keep the needs of European federation in mind in all measures which are undertaken between the end of hostilities and the establishment of peace." The Allied nations should set up a supreme authority for the whole of Europe after the cease-fire, at first under the leadership of the Allies, which would then convene a European Constitutional Assembly as soon as possible.[24] The writings of the Resistance often suggested the advantages of a United Europe to the world powers. As one Dutch author said: The Americans have long found "the constant tensions and wars among the European nations incomprehensible. If Europe now discovers the way to political unity, only one answer can come from America: at last!"[25] An article of the *"Comité Général d'Études"* of the French Resistance tried to quiet Soviet fears by arguing that "the formation of a federated Europe ought to satisfy Russia in every respect, for, in the first place, capitalism would be prevented from entrenching itself on the Continent" and, in the second place, "a lasting peace would be reached on Russia's western borders."[26] People listened with longing for signs that such thoughts were accepted in Allied postwar planning. Churchill's radio message of March 1943 was interpreted in this way. And yet increasingly the Resistance had to report "how the vague feeling persists, that we are not understood by the [Allied] side."[27]

In fact, from the outbreak of the war until the spring of 1943 the thought of regional unions had played an important role in the postwar plans of Great Britain and the United States. The League of Nations, it was argued, had been insufficient; this time one had to create an international organization strong enough to banish once and for all the spirit of national imperialism. In May 1940 the United States Advisory Committee in charge of postwar planning concluded, as a result of Sumner Welles's experiences in Europe, that a peace organization would have the greatest chance of success if various continents would first join together in regional unions which would then form the world peace organization. This idea was shared in Great Britain by influential private associations and individual writers, as well as by Eastern European governments in exile, by committees of parties in exile, and so forth. Churchill himself had in 1940 made the suggestion of an immediate French-British union under a common parliament, and had spoken many times of the "United States of Europe." Again in March 1943, when the counterarguments of the Soviet and American governments were already clear, he had expressed his "hope that, under a world institution embodying . . . all nations, there should come into being a Council of Europe," and had said that the Allies had to succeed in making this council "a really effective League, with all the strongest forces concerned woven into its texture, with a High Court to adjust disputes, and with forces, Armed Forces . . . , held ready to enforce these decisions." Three months later, in Washington, he specified that the future "World Council" could be composed of the three great powers (the Soviet Union, the United States of America, and Great Britain) and representatives of the separate unions of Europe, East Asia, and South America.[28]

But the Soviet leaders had already by the end of 1941 announced quite different plans, plans which derived from their unchanged adherence to the concepts of *Machtpolitik*. They demanded at least the territorial gains which Hitler had offered them in 1939, i.e., the inclusion in the Soviet Union of Estonia, Latvia, the eastern half of Poland, and Bessarabia; and, in addition, of Lithuania and eastern regions of Finland. They recommended that Austria, Bavaria, and the Rhineland, as well as all the traditional national states in Europe, be reconstructed as "sovereign" states. And from the spring of 1942 they rejected with increasing determination any thought of a federation of this multitude of European states in a small area as a "bourgeois movement for intervention against the Soviet Union." Their stand soon revealed itself as one of massive latter-day imperialism. After the victory of Stalingrad in January 1943 had increased the weight of the Soviet Union in the alliance, Stalin developed a diplomatic offensive to carry out this program in the face of Western resistance. He broke off relations with the Polish government in exile, which had been especially inclined toward European federation, seriously threatened to conclude a separate peace with Hitler, and went so far as to recall his ambassadors in London and Washington. Every kind of European federation was criticized by the Moscow press as well as by the communist resistance groups as a brazen threat against the Soviet Union. At the first joint discussion of the foreign ministers in Moscow in October 1943, Molotov refused even to talk about plans for federation.[29]

The decisive factor for Europe's future was that the United States, for extremely complex reasons, accepted this Soviet view. Hull, whose efforts were for a global security organization, felt that continental unions contradicted such a scheme. Roosevelt, who clung to the old idea of "great powers," conceived the idea of the "four world policemen" to whom all smaller states would be subordinated. Convinced that a future peace had to be based on American–Russian cooperation, both Hull and Roosevelt dropped the plans for a European federation and showed their readiness to make concessions also in territorial matters, which were then definitely agreed upon in Teheran in November 1943.[30] The result was that in 1945 the world powers, meeting in the ruins of a destroyed Europe, did nothing more than arrange for the restoration of the system of national states. On the American side, this was done in ignorance of the fact that such a restoration, which contradicted all newly gained European convictions, might result in widespread despair; on the Russian side, with complete awareness of this possibility, and with the expectation that a hopelessly fragmented Europe would now confirm the thesis of the inevitable collapse of the capitalist states. *De facto*, the two world powers divided up the continent into spheres of influence.

The European resistance movements had had no influence upon the Teheran decision. Their programs were probably

unknown to the American statesmen responsible for it. It lay in
the nature of their illegal struggle, which could be waged only in
small groups, that they could not send representatives of the
whole Resistance to meet with the Allies. Now in 1944 they were
gradually seeing how little influence their convictions had had in
fact upon Allied postwar planning. It is moving to hear the cry of
despair that once again "the war had been won, but the peace
lost." For example, one publication of the Dutch Resistance
asserted in 1944 that "we Dutch are Europeans and we believe in
a future for Europe. We do not belong to the Americans, who see
Europe as senile and who from the outset are dividing it up into
an Asiatic and an American sphere of interest. A position for us
as a bridgehead of the West (along with France and Belgium) is
certainly not what we visualize as the final situation."[31] Treated
even ironically was the idea of achieving the new world order
with the great powers as "world policemen," to whom "the
responsibility for this order is given from the outset." Instead one
should anticipate serious tensions among the great powers, which
have to account to no one. Then, "our continent, which as a
political unit could be a bridge between East and West because it
carries both elements in itself, and which as a political power
would contribute to the balance of power in the new League of
Nations, will become a field for parade in peace and a battle-
ground in war." In the end it "will be torn in half and in this
way forced to a development which runs diametrically opposed to
its cultural tradition and its most fundamental economic
needs."[32] And instead of explaining to us how the German
people are "to be taken up into the European community," we
are being told to accept the idea of annexations? We Dutch resistance fighters would rather continue fighting "for our ideal of a
renewed Europe than to attempt to slip between the paws of the
great beasts of prey in order to tear off our own part of the
German cadaver."[33]

It was becoming increasingly evident to Resistance spokesmen
that their programs were in danger of not surviving the European

catastrophe of 1945. Because the planning of the non-communist Resistance no longer coincided with that of the Allies, its actual political value disappeared; some groups abandoned their intellectual leaders, and during the last months of the war parts of the resistance movements degenerated into hatred. Yet no matter how deep the disappointment was, most of those who had been spokesmen up to this time tried to remain faithful to their old ideas, even if it meant for a time to be completely unrealistic. The most astute leaders had long ago anticipated that "in the moment of collapse" of the Nazi system not all powers would automatically unite in a "United States of Europe." They regarded a "federalistic political movement" as a necessity to push the traditional parties beyond their "concerns for the reconstruction of their normal national life," to use their "influence on the masses and to lead them to goals for which they had unconsciously been prepared by the historical developments."[34] They added that the goal of convening a "European constitutional assembly" was further away than they had thought because of the attitude of the Allies; "the way will probably be more devious," but the construction of the "European Federalistic Movement" becomes all the more important.[35] The most significant French Resistance leader, Henri Frenay, summed up this conclusion in these words: "The governments which are in favor of national restorations ought to realize that the necessary decisions will be carried out by their people, and in every country men of the Resistance will be found at their head."[36]

When in 1947 the United States made the historical decision to choose a policy of containment, the Europeans living in the American sphere of influence—almost against historical expectation—received another chance to turn the convictions gained during the Resistance into reality. The leading men of the "Union of European Federalists," who from 1947 to 1956 fought for federative integration in every Western European country with writings, congresses, questionnaires, and pressure groups, were former Resistance leaders. Due to democratic pressure from below and American pressure from above (particularly from the Economic Cooperation Administration), they were in the position of demanding from the restored national governments a series of steps leading toward Western European federation. The main impediment in these ten years was the crucial fact that Great Britain, the four neutral countries, and leading former emigrants, all without direct share in the catastrophic experiences under totalitarian rule, were unable to understand the conclusions which the Resistance on the Continent had drawn from these experiences. The example of Britain, the economic recovery made possible by the Marshall Plan, the beginning of a relaxation of East–West tensions, the increasing strength of national governments on the continent, and de Gaulle's coming to power —all this has helped prevent these governments from taking the decisive step to federation. Since then the European federalists have had no choice but to embrace once again a situation with which they were quite familiar, namely, that of resistance.

The men of the Resistance were risking their lives in opposition to totalitarian rule, not only in the sense of a negative struggle *against* something, but even more, in their opinion, *for* something, for a better and peaceful society. Each group fought against Hitler's dictatorship, not for the old national states—as communist and certain rightist authors of the postwar period have claimed—but rather for a new European society. Although in 1945 their proposals had no prospect of realization, they are nevertheless indicative of a sweeping change in the political thought of a European elite, without which the entire history of Europe since 1945 cannot be understood. We have heard during recent years enough about the failures on the road to European integration, about the crisis and stagnation of European unification. The writings of the Resistance leaders may help us to understand why, despite all these setbacks, the idea of European federation as a long-term trend remains dominant in a considerable proportion of today's European society.

Notes:

[1] The following is the slightly revised text of a lecture presented at a number of American universities in the spring of 1967. I gratefully acknowledge the suggestions of Fritz. T. Epstein, Hajo Holborn, and my colleagues at the Institute for Advanced Study in Princeton during the academic year 1966–67, Felix Gilbert and Peter Paret.

[2] See, for example, all pages under "Europe" in the indexes of H. Rothfels, *Die deutsche Opposition gegen Hitler* (Frankfurt, 1958; enlarged edition of *The German Opposition to Hitler* (Hinsdale, Ill., 1948)) ; H. Michel, *Les Courants de Pensée de la Résistance* (Paris, 1962) ; C. F. Delzell, *Mussolini's Enemies. The Italian Anti-Fascist Resistance* (Princeton, 1961).

[3] See especially C. H. Pegg, "Die Résistance als Träger der europäischen Einigungsbestrebungen in Frankreich des. II. Weltkriegs," *Europa-Archiv*, VII (1952), 5197–206, and Charles F. Delzell, "The European Federalist Movement in Italy: First Phase 1918–1947," *Journal of Modern History*, XXXII (1960), 241–50. I have greatly benefited from these two articles.

[4] Because this *is* a first report, prepared in the form of a lecture, certain difficult areas are necessarily dealt with in a summary and general way. A full account is contained in the author's *Europa-Föderationspläne der Widerstandsbewegungen 1940–1945* (Munich: Oldenbourg, 1968). Footnotes refer (by document number) to this work, in which detailed bibliographical information can be found.

[5] *Op. cit.*, No. 77, Henri Frenay (leader of *Combat*), Dec. 12, 1943.

[6] *Op. cit.*, No. 49, "Kreisauer Grundsatze" (Moltke), Aug. 9, 1943.

[7] *Op. cit.*, No. 17, Mario A. Rollier (editor of the illegal *L'Unità Europea*), May 1944.

[8] *Op. cit.*, No. 81, *Le Franc-tireur, Organe du Mouvement de Libération Nationale*, Edition Sud., Mar. 1, 1944.

[9] *Op. cit.*, No. 10, Foundation Convention of the illegal "Movimento Federalista Europeo," Milan, Aug. 28, 1943.

[10] *Op. cit.*, No. 100, Heuven Goedhart (editor of the illegal *Het Parool*), Dec. 12, 1942.

[11] *Op. cit.*, No. 78, Phillipe Viannay (leader of *Défense de la France*), Jan. 1944.

[12] *Op. cit.*, No. 16, anonymous, in the illegal *L'Unità Europea*, May 1944.

[13] *Op. cit.*, No. 103, anonymous, in *Vrij Nederland*, Sept. 1943.

[14] See for example *op. cit.*, Nos. 50 (Goerdeler) and 62 (O.C.M.), 1942–43.

[15] *Op. cit.*, No. 59, Léon Blum in Riom, June 1942. Cf. Nos. 10, 31, 71, 104, 114a, 129, etc.

[16] *Op. cit.*, No. 11, Luigi Einaudi, illegal leaflet, Sept. 1943.

[17] *Op. cit.*, No. 136, "The Geneva Declaration of Resistants," May 1944.

[18] Both quotations from a "Program" of the *Comité général* of the "Mouvement de Libération Nationale (Région Lyon)," Aug. 1944, *op. cit.*, No. 89.

[19] *Op. cit.*, No. 114, "Program Polski Ludowej," Dec. 1941.

[20] *Op. cit.*, No. 31, Helmuth James Graf von Moltke, "Ausgangslage," Apr. 24, 1941.

[21] *Op. cit.*, No. 100, Heuven Goedhart (Leader of *Het Parool*), Dec. 12, 1942.

[22] *Op. cit.*, No. 10, "Movimento Federalista Europeo," Aug. 28, 1943.

[23] *Op. cit.*, No. 89, "Program," distributed by the *Comité général* of the Mouvement de Libération Nationale (Région Lyon)," Aug. 1944. The leading persons of this committee were socialists. It would be an important task of research to compare the positions of the various authors in domestic and social politics with their convictions concerning the future federation of Europe. The result, so far as I can see, would be that in the great majority European federation plans were written by men of the "left." The "rightists" were either collaborators, or, if they were in the Resistance, would mostly speak in more reserved terms of "confederation" and "collaboration" instead of "federation."

[24] *Op. cit.*, No. 136, "The Geneva Declaration of Resistants," May 1944.

[25] *Op. cit.*, No. 110, "Hades" (H. D. Salinger, The Hague), Sept. 1944.

[26] *Op. cit.*, No. 79, anonymous, in the illegal *Cahiers politiques*, Jan. 1944.

[27] *Op. cit.*, No. 109, Bosch R. van Rosenthal to Willem A. Visser 'tHooft, letter concerning the Geneva Declaration, Aug. 21, 1944.

[28] See with many documents, explanations, differentiations, etc., *op. cit.*, Nos. 139–69.

[29] See in *op. cit.*, especially Nos. 84, 118, 155, 167, 170, and 172. Further research about this attitude of the Soviet Union is needed. To some extent, presumably, it was a continuation of the sort of power politics which saw in the weakness of one's neighbors a guarantee of the welfare of one's own state, but which in the second half of the twentieth century may itself become a cause of weakness. But it is also a continuation of the attitudes of 1929 and 1930, which declared (with some reason) the "European Union" ideas of Briand and Coudenhove to be "bourgeois," "reactionary," and "interventionist." Nevertheless only the former can explain why, with the development of the fascist regimes, the Soviet Union did not accept the fact that conditions had changed.

[30] See also the discussion of the literature (with special reference to William McNeill, Herbert Feis, and Llewellyn Woodward) in *op. cit.*, Nos. 159, 160, 164, 170, and 172.

[31] *Op. cit.*, No. 108, *De Ploeg* (Groningen), Aug. 1944.

[32] *Op. cit.*, No. 110, "Hades" (H. D. Salinger, The Hague), Sept. 1944.

[33] *Op. cit.*, No. 111, A. J. van der Leeuw (in *De Ploeg*), Jan. 1945.

[34] *Op. cit.*, No. 2, Altiero Spinelli for the "Ventotene Group," Aug. 1941.

[35] *Op. cit.*, No. 22, Altiero Spinelli for the "Movimento Federalista Europeo," Sept. 1944.

[36] *Op. cit.*, No. 77, Henri Frenay (Leader of *Combat*), Dec. 12, 1943.

SCHUMAN BREAKS THE DEADLOCK
BY F. ROY WILLIS

The European Coal and Steel Community was the first supra-national organization created in postwar Europe. Although restricted to two sectors of the economy, it was able to demonstrate, as the following excerpt shows, the benefits that could follow from freedom of movement of goods, labor, and capital; and it permitted the creation of the basic institutions of High Authority, Council of Ministers, Common Assembly, and Court of Justice, which could be adapted to the wider union that was to follow with the formation of the European Economic Community six years later. This selection is reprinted from France, Germany, and the New Europe, 1945–1967, *by F. Roy Willis with the permission of the publishers, Stanford University Press. © 1965 and 1968 by the Board of Trustees of the Leland Stanford Junior University.*

On May 9, 1950, Robert Schuman startled his press conference with the announcement that the French government proposed "to place all Franco-German coal and steel production under a common High Authority, in an organization open to the partici-

pation of the other countries of Europe." Pooling of coal and
steel production would "mean the immediate establishment of
common bases of industrial production, which is the first step
toward European Federation and will change the destiny of
regions that have long been devoted to the production of war
armaments of which they themselves have been the constant
victims."[1] The primary motive, however, was not economic, but
political: "to end Franco-German hostility once and for all," as
Schuman wrote later.[2]

Schuman was determined that the world recognize the revolu-
tionary nature, in both aim and method, of the proposal. "Five
years, almost to the day, after the Germans' unconditional surrender," he told the press conference, "France is carrying out the first
decisive act in the construction of Europe, in partnership with
Germany. The situation in Europe will be completely transformed as a result." He then laid down rigid conditions, upon
which the French government would not compromise, for the
establishment of the Community. Such rigorousness emphasized
the urgency and the seriousness of the proposal and was not the
calculated risk it seemed. As Schuman later revealed, his government had already reached "agreement in principle" with the government of Germany.[3]

Thus, with apparent certainty of success, Schuman broke completely with the foreign policy that since Richelieu's time had
been based on the axiom that the weakness of Germany is the
strength of France, and thereby made possible an entirely new
approach to the disputes over the powers of the International
Authority for the Ruhr, of the Military Security Board, and of
the High Commission itself. It put the quarrel over the Saar in a
new setting, and seemed to offer a new solution to the problem of
German rearmament.

THE SCHUMAN PROPOSALS OF MAY 9

The most remarkable feature of the Schuman proposal was the
pre-eminence it gave the so-called functional approach to Euro-

pean unity. The view that European integration should begin in a specific sector of the economy, far from being shockingly new, had been constantly voiced in the preceding months by those who were unhappy with the autarchic organization of European economic life and the Council of Europe's slow progress toward political integration. On April 25, 1949, the Westminster Economic Conference of the European Movement had suggested the creation of European "public institutions" for steel, coal, electricity, and transport as a means of co-ordinating basic industries. On December 13 the Industry Sub-Committee of the Council of Europe's Consultative Assembly had proposed that a public steel authority be given power "to define general policy in the industry, particularly on investment, volume of production, and prices."[4]

For most supporters of such institutions, the final goal was the creation of a common market, if not for all products, at least for selected sectors of industry. In the opening session of the Council of Europe in August 1949, André Philip had attacked the continued pursuit of contradictory national plans of development in a divided and economically unhealthy Europe. Guy Mollet, secretary-general of the French Socialist party, pointed out that the cause of European workers would be best served by "the establishment of a wide, unified market of nearly 300,000,000 people." Edouard Bonnefous (UDSR), president of the Foreign Affairs Commission of the National Assembly, urged the European countries to overcome their unwillingness and "agree to pool their national resources under a joint international administration."[5] Paul Reynaud (Independent) impatiently observed that although "everyone here believes that between the two giants there is a place for Europe, but not for the patchwork of European states," no one was taking the steps necessary to achieve that unity.[6]

For all their impatience, the projects of the "Europeans" seemed unlikely to bear fruit until an impending crisis in the steel industry in the last months of 1949 compelled consideration of them. By 1953, according to the United Nations Economic Commission for Europe, steel consumption in Europe and its overseas markets would reach 62 million tons, and production 70 million, leaving eight million tons of steel without a taker.[7] The Council of Europe warned that balance could be restored "neither by anarchic freedom of national action which would lead rapidly to a crisis, nor by cartelization which would raise production costs, but by harmonizing production and investment in the steel industry."[8] In the summer of 1949 there were signs of falling demand in the steel market, accompanied by pressure of accumulated stocks on prices. Even in the coal industry, there were signs that Europe's penury was nearing an end. The Schuman Plan was conceived in response to imminent overproduction in two basic industries, and was announced to the world some seven weeks before the crossing of the 38th parallel by North Korean troops precipitated the rearmament of Europe and created a vast new market for coal and steel.

The postwar reconstruction of European heavy industry had been undertaken on a national basis, with little or no reference to the needs of Europe as a whole or to a rational division of production according to natural resources and industrial plant. Marshall Aid funds had only increased national economic autarchy; and the Organization for European Economic Co-operation had proved powerless to compel co-ordinated planning. The result had been the development of uneconomic mines and factories, protected by tariff barriers, transport differentials, import quotas, and the like.[9] In no sector of the economy was this irrational development more apparent than in the French coal and steel industry, where highly efficient and modernized plants and mines operated beside smaller units of increasingly obsolescent production methods and low-quality resources. The first necessity for the European coal and steel industries was widely thought to be an international planning authority, with the power to enforce its decisions.

A further problem was the fluctuation of demand in two industries in which vast investment and large-scale production permitted only slow changes in production levels.[10] In the 1920's and 1930's the steel industry had attempted to meet this problem by forming international cartels that divided the market between their members; and there were indications in the summer of 1949 of a new cartel in the making. André Philip noted that "a large number of steel manufacturers of different nationalities have gotten into the habit of meeting and taking tea together. When I see employers in the same industry taking tea together too often, I admit that I begin to get worried. It is not yet a cartel; nevertheless, these are already contacts, preliminary negotiations."[11] The second need, therefore, that the Schuman Plan was intended to meet, was for an institution other than a cartel to safeguard both producer and consumer against fluctuations of the business cycle.

Finally, production was planned within the restrictions of national frontiers. Markets, demarcated by national borders, were divided up as irrationally as production. Only a large market and the free passage of goods to their most rational outlet would make specialization and large-scale production possible.

There were thus persuasive, if not irrefutable, economic arguments for the establishment of some new international organization for the European coal and steel industries. Few people suspected that the blueprint of just such an organization was being prepared, in utmost secrecy, in the offices of the Commissariat du Plan de Modernisation et d'Equipement. On the Rue de Martignac, Jean Monnet, the head of the Commissariat, and a handful of his closest collaborators were drawing up the plan that would bear Schuman's name. They worked alone. "The administrative departments were not consulted, nor the Quai d'Orsay, nor the Ministry of Industrial Production, nor that of National Defense. The directors of the coal mines and of the iron and steel industry were not consulted either. Parliament was not forewarned."[12] Only on the morning of May 9 was the French cabinet asked to approve the proposal. Monnet believed that secrecy and speed were essential, that surprise would permit an appeal over the heads of governments to European citizens anxious for some positive step toward integration. He was determined that the plan would not be the result of compromise between political groups or sectional interests, but would be presented in exactly the form in which it had been conceived. It is now fairly clear that, in the preparation of the plan, Pierre Uri, one of Monnet's chief assistants at the Commissariat, was responsible for the economic sections; Paul Reuter, a law professor at Aix-en-Provence, for the final legal presentation; and Jacques Gascuel, editor of *Perspectives*, for the preamble.[13] But the guiding ideas and the tone of the whole document were Monnet's.

With the preparation of this plan for the creation of the European Coal and Steel Community (ECSC), Monnet became the central figure in the European integration movement. Whereas Robert Schuman was pre-eminently the man of the invasion frontier, whose overriding interest was Franco-German reconciliation, Monnet's varied career in private business and international economics had given him wider aims. He worked for his father's cognac firm (J. G. Monnet and Co.) in western Canada before the First World War, and managed the company between 1923 and 1925. During the war, he worked in the French Ministry of Commerce on Anglo-French supply questions and afterward became deputy secretary-general of the League of Nations. In the inter-war years, he had been all over the world—Peking, New York, Stockholm, Warsaw—primarily as economic adviser to foreign governments with a wide assortment of economic problems. The Second World War found him in London, as representative of the Reynaud government, where he inspired Churchill's proposal for Anglo-French union.[14] Churchill sent him to Washington to work on Allied supply planning, but in 1943 he joined de Gaulle in Algiers and became a member of the CFLN. In 1945, he was named head of the Commissariat executing the national modernization plan, of which he was the principal author.[15]

From this extraordinarily varied experience, Monnet had

drawn several lessons. He believed that only exposure to foreign competition would bring about rationalization of French production methods; that "the creation of a large internal market is indispensable to make it possible for Europeans to take their place in the world again"; and that the final aim of such a market should be nothing less than a United States of Europe.[16] In all his speeches Monnet emphasized that Europe must follow the example of the United States, whose common market of 160 million inhabitants he regarded as the primary cause of American economic productivity. The Europe he conceived of was not a small, inner group, but the union of all the free nations of the West, including, above all, Britain.

Monnet was, therefore, by experience and belief oriented toward Britain and the Atlantic alliance, and he turned to Germany for practical reasons. According to those close to him in 1950, he was convinced that the danger of war made immediate steps toward European economic unity imperative. The coal and steel industries were not an obvious choice, economically; more modernized industries would have involved fewer technical problems and more receptive managers and owners. Monnet chose these industries, the basis of war production, for their psychological importance; their internationalization would be an unquestionable step toward the political unity of Europe. "Our Community," Monnet told the Council of Europe on March 28, 1953, "is not an association of producers of coal and steel; it is the beginning of Europe."[17]

After failing to interest Premier Bidault in the plan at the beginning of May, Monnet approached the foreign minister, Robert Schuman, with whom he had established close ties when Schuman was minister of finance. Schuman agreed to bring the proposal before the cabinet and to make it public before the coming conference of the three Western foreign ministers. Several days of hectic activity in the Commissariat offices followed. On May 4, Bernard Clappier, Schuman's *chef de cabinet*, Gascuel, Uri, and Etienne Hirsch together drew up the Plan's introductory chapter, as well as two notes refuting anticipated objections to it. On May 8, all preparatory papers were burned. On May 9, at 10 A.M., Clappier brought the final text to Schuman, and it was approved by the cabinet in the early afternoon. Schuman was thus able to present the proposal to over a hundred newsmen at four o'clock that afternoon, gaining, as Monnet had hoped, the advantages of total surprise.

For Schuman, this press conference was the climax of his career, the moment for which his whole life had prepared him. For him "Franco-German reconciliation was not a decision of the intellect, but of the heart." Unlike many in Lorraine and Alsace, he had reacted to suffering at German hands not by withdrawing into Germanophobic nationalism, but by rising above nationalism. His family was originally from Evrange in Lorraine, but after fighting against Prussia in 1871, his father moved to Luxembourg, where Robert Schuman was born in 1886. He studied at the universities of Bonn, Munich, and Berlin, but took his doctorate at the University of Strasbourg in 1910. In 1912 he was admitted to the bar at Metz. During the First World War he was drafted into the German Army. Only in 1919, at the age of thirty-three, did he finally become a French citizen.

On November 16, 1919, he was elected deputy for the Moselle, a seat he retained, except during the Second World War, until 1960. In parliament he continued to be occupied with the affairs of Alsace as president of the Commission for Alsace-Lorraine from 1928 to 1936. He first entered the French cabinet when Paul Reynaud named him under-secretary for refugees in March 1940, and he followed the Pétain government to Vichy, where he voted to grant the marshal supreme powers. He quickly broke with Pétain, however, resigned his post, and returned to his home in Metz. There he was arrested by the Gestapo, held prisoner in a cellar for months, and finally deported to Germany. For seven months, he was imprisoned in Neustadt in the Pfalz, but after release under supervision, he made his way to France in August 1942. After the Germans took over Vichy France in November, he again became a fugitive, hiding out in convents and working with the Resistance. In a bitter epilogue to these war years, he found himself accused of collaboration as a member of the Pétain cabinet, but all charges against him were thrown out.[18]

In postwar France, Schuman became a major figure in the Christian Democratic MRP, which he had helped found in 1944. At first he returned to his primary interest, finance, in the 1946 Bidault government. But as Premier (November 24, 1947–July 19, 1948) and foreign minister (almost continuously from July 26, 1948, to December 23, 1952) he found himself in a position to shape French foreign policy to his vision of a Europe in which France and Germany were reconciled and the suffering of the border provinces ended. He presided over the government that abandoned the French thesis and accepted the London Agreements of June 1948. As foreign minister, he brought France into the Atlantic Pact, and at the same time accepted the Washington Agreements on the future High Commission. After a few hours' conversation with Duncan Sandys, the secretary of the United Europe movement, he agreed to sponsor the European parliamentary assembly which became the Council of Europe.[19]

With the same decisiveness, he agreed to Monnet's request that he sponsor the proposed Coal and Steel Community. He realized that Monnet's proposal offered that new approach to the tangled problem of Franco-German relations for which many statesmen had been groping. The fiasco of his trip through Germany in January had made him more determined than ever to find a solution at once practical and idealistic. He knew, however, that as a onetime German he would be accused of sacrificing French interests to Germany, and he was to feel these accusations deeply. Nevertheless, he made the proposal his own, and presented it with a sincerity and lack of rhetorical flourish that made it all the more impressive. Schuman himself was quite clear what his order of priorities would be. While the final aim was European federation, he realized that "Europe will not be created in one stroke nor in one operation, but by concrete achievements that will

create a sound basis from the start"—namely, the elimination of
the "ancient antagonism of France and Germany" through
"establishment of common bases of industrial production."

The detailed organization of the new Community was
described in Schuman's first announcement, since, as he wrote
later, "its planners had, from the very first, a precise picture of
the projected system; at the same time, they spelled out its objectives, its means, and its procedure, with a rigidity that surprised
and sometimes shocked those accustomed to greater suppleness in
diplomacy."[20] A supranational High Authority, consisting of
"independent persons," chosen by the member governments but
responsible to the Community as a whole, was to modernize production and improve quality, supply coal and steel "on identical
terms" to France, Germany, and other participating countries, to
develop common export markets in other countries, and to raise
the living standards of workers in these countries. The methods
recommended included a plan of investment and production,
price equalization measures and a fund to aid rationalization of
production, and the end of all customs duties and import quotas.

The surprise seemed to have produced the desired results,
except in England, where the government reacted to surprises
from the Continent with traditional distrust, and on May 27
rejected the invitation to join the new Community. In the
United States, the proposal was greeted with immediate approval
in all circles. Chancellor Adenauer, who had learned of the proposal only that morning in a personal letter from Schuman,
approved the main lines of the Plan despite the surprise. Italy,
Belgium, Luxembourg, and the Netherlands accepted the basic
principles of the Plan; and the six governments announced the
opening of a conference on June 20 for the purpose of drafting
the treaty that would create the European Coal and Steel
Community. The conference met for nine months of arduous,
technical work. The final treaty, by then ninety pages long, was
initialed on March 15, 1951, signed on April 18, 1951, and
after ratification in the six national parliaments came into force
on July 25, 1952.

The two-year period between the announcement of May 9, 1950, and the establishment of the Coal and Steel Community was of necessity marked in France and Germany by stock-taking of relative economic positions, as well as by sometimes hard-headed, sometimes emotional attempts to forecast the relative advantages and disadvantages of the new Community. Different sectors of opinion in each country envisaged the effects of the Plan from their particular economic, political, and emotional standpoints. Special-interest groups sought to bring pressure upon public opinion and the men who would ratify the treaty. For much of the time, as the struggle raged, the future of the Community remained in doubt.

THE ECONOMICS OF RAPPROCHEMENT

Although Schuman had promised that his Plan would make "any war between France and Germany not only unthinkable, but materially impossible," and would be the "first step toward European Federation," the immediate appeal of the Plan rested on his claim that "establishment of common bases of economic development" would bring major economic advantages to both France and Germany—a claim that was to be vehemently debated. One group held that "in spite of myths, Franco-German hostility never had an essentially economic cause. Whatever the frontier lines, the industries of Lorraine and the Ruhr have always traded together (coal against steel) and come to an understanding."[21] Removal of trade barriers between the two countries was desirable, because their coal and steel industries were complementary rather than competitive. Others maintained that, in a common market in coal and steel, essentially similar and competitive industries would confront each other. This group, which included Monnet and his collaborators, held that competition within a large common market would permit large-scale production, specialization by region and industry, rationalization of outlets, and the most productive use of capital and labor. The well-being of the Community as a whole would further the well-being of each individual member.

French opponents of the Schuman Plan argued that a common market of countries of essentially similar economic structure would simply sacrifice the weaker industries and regions to the stronger, and eventually lead to German economic and political hegemony. "Tomorrow, if the optimistic views of M. Monnet are realized," Alfred Krieger (RPF) told the National Assembly, "Germany will be the major exporter of coal to France, Germany the major exporter of iron and steel products to France and the French Union, Germany the major exporter of manufactured goods to the same territories, Germany a minor consumer of Lorraine ore. . . . Listen to me: one should not tempt the devil."[22] Faced with these conflicting forecasts of the effect of a common market in coal and steel, government and private groups in both France and Germany began a thorough analysis of their relative economic positions. While the analysis increased rather than diminished anxieties in both French and German industrial circles, it at least destroyed many popular oversimplifications.

The report of the French Conseil Economique on the Schuman Plan noted that for 1949–50 France's coal requirements were 62 million tons, whereas 1949 production was only 51.2 million tons. In 1949 Saar production was 14.3 million tons and its consumption 5 million tons, leaving a surplus apparently sufficient to meet anticipated French requirements of 70 million tons per year. However, in 1950 and 1951 France imported an average of 6,468,000 tons from Germany, and an average of only 764,000 from the Saar.[23] This dependence on German imports is explained by the inferior quality of French and Saar coal; unless mixed with large quantities of high-grade Ruhr coal, it was unsuitable for coking and hence for the production of steel. The most important fact of Franco-German economic relations was France's reliance upon Germany for over 10 per cent of its coal.

The regional differences among French coal-producing areas were also to be significant in the new Community. France's coal mines were located mainly in three major areas—the Nord/Pas-de-Calais, Lorraine, and the Centre/Midi. Northern France has been called a small-scale Ruhr because it is the only area in France that produced both coal of coking quality and iron ore. Nevertheless, its production costs were so high in comparison with the Ruhr's (the pithead price was $2.76 a ton higher) that free competition with the Ruhr was expected to lead to the abandonment of 20 to 25 per cent of its productive capacity and to the unemployment of about 40,000 miners.[24] The Centre/Midi, with mines of more marginal productivity, supplied only the local market, on which its locational, and hence price, advantage protected it from Ruhr competition. Lorraine produced only 9.8 million tons of coal in 1949, and of that only 13 per cent was fit for coking.[25] According to Jean Chardonnet, "In all, from purely French sources the Lorraine steel industry had only 1,714,000 tons of coke at its disposal when it needed 6,816,000."[26] Clearly, the problem of French dependence on German coke came down to the dependence of Lorraine on Germany. Since Lorraine produced 65.5 per cent of French steel, this meant that for three days out of four, it was dependent upon coal and coke from the Ruhr. The price to be paid for the free flow of Ruhr coal and coke to Lorraine and the supply of cheap German coal to other regions could be to abandon over 25 per cent of France's mining capacity and to throw between 40,000 and 50,000 French miners out of work.

Germany had no coal shortage, since the Ruhr produced not only half the coal in the Community, but three-quarters of the coking coal. About 10 per cent of the Ruhr's primary coal was for export. In minor markets like south Germany, French coal competed with the Ruhr's, and even this slight challenge was enough to make certain German coal producers hesitate to enter the Community. The question at issue in the German coal industry (which traditionally had been vertically integrated with steel production) was whether the free flow of German coal and coke to other European countries, especially France, would reduce the supply available to the German steel industry and thus enable foreign steel to compete with German, or whether German mining

Table 1/ Comparative Efficiency and Costs in German and French Mines, 1949[27]

Country/Mine	Output (Million Tons)	Output per Man Shift (Tons)	Labor Costs ($ per Ton)	Operating Costs ($ per Ton)[a]	Pithead Price ($ per Ton)[b]
WEST GERMANY	103.2	1.03	3.76	6.66	7.19
FRANCE	65.6	0.72	6.13	8.22	9.37
Nord	27.7	0.64	6.88	8.74	9.95
Lorraine	9.8	0.96	5.21	6.62	7.54
Blanzy	2.6	0.87	5.06	6.43	7.33
Loire	3.8	0.73	5.60	7.11	8.10
Auvergne	1.2	0.67	6.72	8.53	9.74
Cévennes	2.9	0.59	7.76	9.85	11.23
Aquitaine	2.0	0.72	6.31	8.01	9.14
Dauphiné	0.5	0.60	8.15	10.35	11.80
Saar	14.2	0.85	5.27	8.48	9.50

[a]Approximate totals.   [b]Estimated prices.

interests would ultimately profit from an assured market for their abundant production. Opinion remained divided in Germany, especially during the High Commission's attempt to abolish the vertical ties of coal and steel in Germany.[28]

The French steel industry, too, was centered in the Nord/Pas-de-Calais, Lorraine, and Centre/Midi regions, although there were several minor steel-producing regions dependent upon electric power, such as the Alpine region, or at tidewater, such as Rouen and Caen.[29] Again there was great disparity of production. Lorraine accounted for 65.5 per cent of French steel production and 78 per cent of French pig iron. While Lorraine had ample iron ore, however, it was low in iron content (about 30 per cent), and required large quantities of coke for producing steel by the Thomas process. In 1955, Lorraine produced 46.7 million tons of iron ore, and the Centre/Midi another 3.6 million. The Nord/Pas-de-Calais produced very little. France imported 547,000 tons, compared with a total home production of 50,326,000,[30] and was therefore only marginally dependent upon foreign ore supplies.

In fact, France was a major exporter of iron ore. In 1949, France accounted for over 70 per cent of the ore production of the future Community and exported 22 per cent of its production (7.2 million tons), largely to Belgium and Luxembourg. Germany, however, was only to the slightest degree dependent upon iron ore from Lorraine. Although Lorraine ore had supplied a quarter of the Ruhr's needs before 1914, after the return of Lorraine to France the Ruhr had completely changed its sources of supply, of which Sweden was now the most important. Although the Conseil Economique concluded with the hope that the Schuman Plan would re-establish the traditional exchange of coal for iron ore between the Ruhr and Lorraine, this did not happen; as late as 1955, Germany was importing from France only 364,000 tons of iron ore out of total imports of 14,314,000 tons.[31] The chance of increasing iron-ore sales to Germany inside the Community was not a persuasive argument for French industry, in spite of propaganda claims, nor was access to Lorraine supplies of great appeal to German industry.

More significant was the competition of the two countries for markets. Fear of German competition was evident in French insistence upon a low ceiling of steel production in Germany and the execution of the dismantling and deconcentration programs. The competition was especially bitter because the extreme fluctuation of the European steel market made it difficult to co-ordinate the immense investments involved in steel production with future demands.[32]

Both French and German iron and steel producers found their main markets at home. The minor producing areas of France generally supplied the local market. The Centre/Midi supplied the producers of ordnance, machine tools, and engineering equipment in the area, especially large companies such as Schneider. The Nord/Pas-de-Calais sold 41 per cent of its steel locally, 20 per cent in the area between the Channel and Paris, and only 14 per cent abroad. The main concern in the Nord, therefore, was that cheaper German steel would infiltrate its most important market in Paris and the northeast. Lorraine lacked local markets, only 13 per cent of its steel staying in the region and 33 per cent being exported from France.[33] Lorraine therefore had two worries in the market: first, normal competition with a growing German steel industry, in which it might be aided by cheaper coal and by market regulation inside the Community; second, the potential threat of German steel to its domestic market. The second was particularly important, since the French steel industry was working at only 85 per cent of capacity in 1949 and was already losing its prewar market because of high costs and almost exclusive concentration on the home market since 1945.

The Conseil Economique concluded that free competition with Germany inside the Community would endanger certain sectors of the steel industry: "In reality, there are as many problems as factories." On evidence supplied by the Ministry of Industry, it predicted difficulties for about 13 per cent of the factories producing cast iron, four factories in all; eight of twenty steel factories of less than 100,000-ton capacity, accounting for 3.7 per cent of total production; 26 of 46 processing factories, representing about 10 per cent of production, which, in fact, were already in trouble in 1949. Steel factories producing more than 100,000 tons were expected to compete successfully.[34]

The German steel industry, potentially far stronger than the French, feared the opening of the coal and steel pool because of dismantling (which it claimed had destroyed 25 per cent of its productive capacity); interruption of investment during the occupation; possible severance of the vertical ties of the coal and steel industries; and deconcentration, which had dispersed the efficient productive units of prewar Germany. German steel men held that, as a result of the favored position the French steel industry had enjoyed under the modernization plan from 1947 to

1949, French steel might infiltrate the south German market. The German producers with most to fear from strong foreign competition were those of the isolated Watenstedt-Salzgitter region, where little steel was consumed locally. The Ruhr producers feared that easy access to the Ruhr's highly developed water-transport system would enable the French to penetrate the German home market, and for that reason opposed construction of the Moselle canal.

The relative situation of the French and German coal and steel industries in 1949 can be summarized as follows:

1. France required large imports of coking coal and coke, especially for the steel mills of Lorraine, obtainable chiefly from the Ruhr. This dependence was France's chief economic interest in a common market in coal and steel.

2. About a quarter of Germany's coal exports went to France, by far the most important foreign customer of the Ruhr mines. German mining groups were therefore interested in guaranteed access to French markets. Increase of German coal sales in France would, however, imply the closing of uneconomical French mines in the Nord/Pas-de-Calais and the Centre/Midi.

3. France exported a significant proportion of its iron ore, but only a negligible amount to Germany. It is incorrect to speak of a two-way traffic—iron ore vs. coal. An increase of French ore exports to Germany was welcomed neither in France (because of limited deposits of ore) nor in Germany (because of the poor quality of French ore).

4. Germany exported a small quantity of steel to France, and France to Germany. Neither country was dependent upon the other for steel, but rather feared competition in both the home and the export markets. France feared the enormous potential of German steel production, Germany the immediate lead of the French.

There was thus one immediate economic benefit promised by the pool, French access to the coal and coke of the Ruhr, and one immediate hardship, the closing down of the most uneconomical producers in each country.

Notes:

[1] Schuman's short introduction and the text are given in Pierre Gerbert's important article, "La Genèse du Plan Schuman: Des Origines à la déclaration du 9 mai 1950," *Revue française de science politique*, July–Sept. 1956, pp. 525–53.

[2] Paul Reuter, *La Communauté Européenne du Charbon et de l'Acier* (Paris, 1953), p. 4, for which Schuman wrote an introduction.

[3] *Ibid.*; Robert Schuman, *Pour l'Europe* (Paris, 1963), pp. 106–8, 153–75.

[4] André Philip, *L'Europe unie et sa place dans l'économie internationale* (Paris, 1953), pp. 200–2; France, Conseil économique, *Communauté Européenne du Charbon et de l'Acier* (Etudes et Travaux No. 21; Paris, 1950), p. 5.

[5] Council of Europe, *Debates*, Aug. 16, 1949, pp. 78–81; Aug. 17, 1949, pp. 158–61; Aug. 23, 1949, pp. 274–79. See also Edouard Bonnefous, *L'Europe en face de son destin* (Paris, 1955), p. 159, and Edouard Bonnefous, *L'Idée européenne et sa réalisation* (Paris, 1950).

[6] Council of Europe, *Debates*, Aug. 23, 1949, p. 261.

[7] United Nations Organization, Economic Commission for Europe, Steel Division, *Evolution et perspectives de la sidérurgie européenne* (Geneva, 1949), p. 75.

[8] Bonnefous, *L'Europe en face*, p. 160; Henri Rieben, *Des Ententes de maîtres de forges au Plan Schuman* (Lausanne, 1954), p. 314.

[9] Richard Mayne, *The Community of Europe* (New York, 1963), pp. 75–78.

[10] France, Conseil économique, *Communauté Européenne du Charbon et de l'Acier*, p. 12.

[11] France, Assemblée nationale, *Débats*, July 26, 1950, p. 5940. On the cartels of the interwar years, see Louis Lister, *Europe's Coal and Steel Community: An Experiment in Economic Union* (New York, 1960), pp. 181–94.

[12] Gerbert, "La Genèse du Plan Schuman," *Revue française de science politique*, July–Sept. 1956, p. 546.

[13] *Ibid.*, pp. 541–43; Mayne, *Community of Europe*, p. 90.

[14] *Time*, Oct. 6, 1961, pp. 28–33: Alfred Grosser, *La IVe République et sa politique extérieure* (Paris, 1961), pp. 59–60.

[15] *L'Année politique, 1944–1945*, pp. 6, 32, 116, 127, 386–87.

[16] Jean Monnet, *Les Etats-Unis d'Europe ont commencé: Discours et allocutions, 1952–1954* (Paris, 1955), pp. 29, 46–47, 51-52.

[17] *Ibid.*, p. 65. Cf. Jean Monnet, 'A Ferment of Change,' *Journal of Common Market Studies*, April 1963, pp. 203–11.

[18] *Neue Zürcher Zeitung*, Sept. 5, 1963, Sept. 6, 1963; *Frankfurter Allgemeine Zeitung*, Sept. 5, 1963; *Le Monde*, Sept. 5, 1963, Sept. 6, 1963.

[19] See the article on the death of Robert Schuman by Jacques de Bourbon-Busset, Schuman's *directeur de cabinet* from 1948 to 1952, "Un Homme droit, Robert Schuman," *Le Monde*, Sept. 6, 1963.

[20] Reuter, *Communauté Européenne du Charbon et de l'Acier*, p. 3.

21 *Manchester Guardian*, May 30, 1950.

22 France, Assemblée nationale, *Débats*, Dec. 7, 1951, pp. 8911–13.

23 France, Conseil économique, *Communauté Européenne du Charbon et de l'Acier*, p. 7; Lister, *Europe's Coal and Steel Community*, pp. 445, 440.

24 K. K. F. Zawadzki, "The Economics of the Schuman Plan," *Oxford Economic Papers* (New Series), V (June 1953), No. 2, pp. 157–89.

25 Lister, *Europe's Coal and Steel Community*, pp. 32, 37f.

26 Jean Chardonnet, *La Sidérurgie française: Progrès ou décadence?* (Paris, 1954), p. 74.

27 United Nations Organization, Economic Commission for Europe, *Economic Bulletin for Europe*, II, No. 2, p. 27, cited by Zawadzki, *Oxford Economic Papers* (New Series), V (June 1953), No. 2, pp. 158–59.

28 Lister, *Europe's Coal and Steel Community*, pp. 24–28. Institut zur Förderung öffentlicher Angelegenheiten, *Was Steckt dahinter?* (Frankfurt am Main, n.d.), pp. 23–24, points out that German mines have much to gain in having a ready market for their production.

29 Chardonnet, *Sidérurgie française*, gives useful map of location of French steel factories. See also the brochure of the Chambre Syndicale de la Sidérurgie Française, *La Sidérurgie en France* (Paris, n.d.).

30 Lister, *Europe's Coal and Steel Community*, pp. 431–47.

31 France, Conseil économique, *Communauté Européenne du Charbon et de l'Acier*, p. 40.

32 Horst Carl Hahn, *Der Schuman-Plan* (Munich, 1953), pp. 19–23.

33 Lister, *Europe's Coal and Steel Community*, pp. 34–37.

34 France, Conseil économique, *Communauté Européenne du Charbon et de l'Acier*, pp. 128–31.

35 Henry W. Ehrmann, "The French Trade Associations and the Ratification of the Schuman Plan," *World Politics*, July 1954, pp. 456–57, and Henry W. Ehrmann, *Organized Business in France* (Princeton, 1957), pp. 368–419.

36 *Ibid.*, pp. 320–24, 380. Ehrmann cites the figure of one billion francs from *Esprit*, January 1949.

THE DEFEAT OF THE EUROPEAN ARMY
BY HENRI BRUGMANS

The rejection of the treaty instituting a European Defense Community by the French parliament on August 30, 1954, destroyed the momentum of the first, federalist phase of the European integration movement. Henri Brugmans, himself a leading federalist and former rector of the College of Europe in Bruges, places French actions in the wider context of its defeat in Indochina, its search for a new relationship with West Germany, and its internal political fragmentation. This chapter originally appeared in "L'Idée européenne, 1920–1970," Cahiers de Bruges, No. 26 (Bruges, 1970), pp. 188–98. It is reprinted here by permission of the journal and the author. The translation is by Helen Baz.

THE FRENCH NATIONAL CRISIS

There was still another reason for the French rejection of the EDC, and it was undoubtedly the main reason: France was then on the brink of great changes and, consequently, was going through a period of anxiety. It sensed that a national crisis was approaching. It no longer had confidence in itself and was fearful of embarking on any new adventures, clinging to an antiquated nationalism.

The public rarely boasted any longer of the glory and grandeur of the mother country. Or if it did, it was done hesitantly, and the clarion call had a false ring to it. It was more concerned about the difficult days ahead. The European Movement suffered from this, since it could flourish only in a climate of daring and virility. How are we going to stand up to German competition? the French asked themselves. How can we avoid being submerged, in an international army, by Germanic dynamism, which we know so well? Above all, how can we create European union without giving up our old ways, good or bad, to which, rightly or wrongly, we are so attached . . . ?

In short, the France of those years resembled only too closely the image drawn of it by the Swiss historian Herbert Lüthy in his book *Frankreichs Uhren gehen anders;*[1] or the description given by a Frenchman who, later on, was to direct the Paris services of the Community: François Fontaine in his essay *La Nation Frein.* There is a lot of material worth quoting from this essay if only to measure the difference between the France of those years and of later ones. In particular, the section entitled "Le Musée Français et ses Conservateurs" contains a passage which aptly sums up the "neophobia" which, at that time, seemed to characterize a nation which, although already in the process of transforming its economy, remained, politically, at the level of a declining artisanship.

Should we revolutionize the universe? Of course! So long as our traditional institutions remain untouched! Should we build a new Europe? If need be, although it is too modest an ambition, since we should be uniting the whole world! Whatever happens, we must move forward—providing that none of our privileges, none of our inefficiencies, none of our protectionism, is threatened because of it.

For the Frenchman sees progress solely in terms of a perpetual credit with positive balances being carried forward to the top of the page. If progress were to deprive him of a single profit, if it were to remove any advantage already won, it would no longer be progress. Once having established this dogma, he is quite prepared to build a new Europe while retaining nationalism, to produce cheaper goods so long as costly enterprises remain untouched, to grant more rights to native peoples while giving up none of his own.

There may be more reactionary people than the French. There is none more conservative.[2]

The Treaty itself was open to many different criticisms. It had been drawn up to resolve a number of problems concurrently, and, consequently, antagonized a wide spectrum of views and exposed itself to attack from all quarters.

It was President Antoine Pinay who most aptly described this multiplicity of aims pursued by the EDC. On 19 March 1953, at the Congress of Independents and Peasants, he admitted that the authors of the Treaty had drafted an unbalanced document, since they had sought to find one single formula to "achieve European security, German rearmament and a step in the organization of Europe at the same time."[3] This apparent error of logic was another cause for criticism by France.

Certainly, it would have been difficult to do more or, *rebus sic stantibus*, to do less. The fact remains that the Treaty, as it stood, aroused the anger of a large number of people: the anti-militarists (who were not necessarily anti-European); the anti-Americans (who had possibly dreamed of a politically constituted "European" Europe); the anti-Germans (who, nevertheless, were perhaps "pro-Atlantic" because of anti-Bolshevism)—to say nothing of the romantic nationalists who believed in "France only," and the communists. It was, undoubtedly, an ill-assorted coalition which formed the majority on 30 August 1954.

Finally, in a France suffering from such doubts, the campaign for this vulnerable Treaty was ineffective and ill-conceived. The federalists realized the danger threatening them when it was already too late, and even then their tactics were hesitant and uncertain.

To succeed, as already mentioned, they should have chosen one of two alternatives: either present the EDC as the best way to contain an ever-dangerous "eternal" Germany—or else base all their arguments on the idea of European fraternity, mutual trust and the prospect of a federalist future. The "Europeans," however, combined both these arguments, which were, sentimentally, incompatible.

Under these circumstances, they were outmaneuvered. They tried their best but fought the campaign as if they had something to be ashamed of. Forced into a defensive posture, they faltered. Victory rarely goes to those who go into battle downhearted, lacking complete conviction and internally divided.[4]

Could the situation have taken a different turn "if" . . . ? The question is hypothetical. The fact remains that most of the political parties of the Fourth Republic lost a lot of their homogeneity in the EDC quarrel and, consequently, much of their prestige in the eyes of the public. The régime itself was discredited because of its vacillation and doubts over this crucial problem.

Since the French public was given virtually no guidance by their leaders, they became more and more confused about the Plan. Few people believed that the military sphere was more suitable than other areas for Franco-German collaboration: why not explore all the other possibilities first, especially economic cooperation? There was something to be said for this suggestion but, unfortunately, the government had no choice in the matter, for the defense problem was urgent since the Korean invasion.

Strangely enough, the number of "don't knows" increased rather than decreased as the debate developed, and at the time of the final crisis had reached a level of 35 per cent compared with 32 per cent in favor of the Treaty or "more or less in favor" and 33 against or "more or less against."[5] These figures are a clear indication of the confused state of public opinion.

Two arguments apparently played a decisive part in making up people's minds: "Could the Germans be trusted?" and "Was there any reason to fear a Soviet military threat?" Opinions fluctuated considerably on these two questions, but the very terminology of the first one showed clearly that the whole problem had been badly put. In July 1954, 56 per cent of the people interviewed thought that "it would be dangerous to rearm Germany in any form whatsoever," and although this was certainly an understandable reaction, it ignored the fact that the EDC claimed, in fact, to be an alternative to the national rearmament of West Germany. Nevertheless, the pollsters were probably quite right to put their question in this way since, as far as the public was concerned, there was no other way of putting it. In other words, the opinion polls were a true reflection of the confused state of mind of the public.

Only two of the political parties joined wholeheartedly in the debate without any second thoughts. The Mouvement Républicain Populaire was virtually unanimous in its support of the Treaty with only a very small number of defectors.[6] Of course the Communist party members all voted without exception against the Treaty. Yet, in both these cases, this unanimity in the top ranks of the parties did not correspond exactly to the opinions of the rank and file members, and even less so among the electorate. Among communist supporters, 16 per cent abstained and, even more surprising, 6 per cent were in favor or "more or less in favor" of the treaty. On the other hand, 11 per cent of MRP supporters were against the Treaty.

In other parties, the figures clearly reflect the inner contradictions which were in evidence throughout the country. Among the socialists, 35 per cent were in favor or "more or less in favor" and 38 per cent against or "more or less" against, while, among the Gaullists, these proportions were reversed—38 per cent in favor and 36 per cent against. The radicals seemed more in favor since 44 per cent were in favor and 33 against, while the EDC received its strongest support from the moderates: 60 per cent in favor and only 11 per cent against.

Sharp and often bitter words were exchanged between the leaders of all these parties. Each group found arguments in its doctrine to support the EDC case, side by side with equally pertinent arguments against.

Among the left, the fear of a "helmeted" Germany, believed as always to be potentially aggressive, militarist and anti-Semitic, vied with the old internationalist instinct which attracted them to European federalism. But at the same time they were haunted by another fear, that of a "Vaticanized" Europe. After all, the three main architects of Europe—Schuman, Adenauer and De Gasperi—were all Catholics. Nevertheless, it would have been difficult to detect any "Roman" influence in the policies of these Christian Democrats who had all adopted independent postures vis-à-vis the ecclesiastical hierarchy. It could even be said that the MRP had never gone to such lengths not to appear as a "clerical" party. Yet this was one of the reasons for left-wing mistrust.

The main objection of the socialists, however, was the prospect of an exclusively continental Europe, excluding Great Britain. Although the British Labour party had made it clear that it was extremely suspicious of any kind of European union whatsoever, combined with the fact that they were no longer in power during the debate on the EDC, there was always the hope that they might be returned to power again and that they might be converted to federalism. Furthermore, their future participation would also automatically involve the participation of the Scandinavian Social Democrats—a further reinforcement to progressive forces—from which a Europe of the Six would inevitably be cut off.

The arguments put forward by Guy Mollet should be seen within this context—a man who was not, however, against supranational solutions—when, on 12 February 1952, he spoke to a parliamentary group of the SFIO as follows:

"Let us be quite clear. Given a choice between the possibility of a so-called Europe 'of Charlemagne' and a broader union to include Great Britain, we would have no hesitation in deciding. Our answer is a categorical and definitive '*no*' to the Little Europe. On the other hand, we have great hopes of a union with the United Kingdom."[7]

In fact, the anti-EDC-ists formed the majority in the socialist group in the National Assembly, whereas in the Executive Committee of the party, they were in the minority and were even threatened with expulsion. But how could they expel several dozen deputies?

Among radical parliamentarians, the majority was also opposed to the Treaty, and in the final stages, the intervention of Edouard Herriot, while not altogether unexpected, influenced, nonetheless, certain undecided members. Yet, the official spokesman of Republic orthodoxy could scarcely be accused of chauvinism. When opposing the nationalist policy of Poincaré, he had constantly lent his support to the League of Nations and, in January 1925, he had made a pathetic speech in the Chamber, certain passages of which had had widespread repercussions: "My greatest wish is to see one day the creation of the United States of Europe. And if I have courageously devoted all my efforts to supporting the League of Nations—I have the right to say this—it is because I saw the first rough outline of these United States of Europe in this great institution."[8] Five years later, he even published a book called *Europe*, whose originality was questionable but whose direction was clearly towards federation. The present attitude of the president of the Assembly against the EDC was, therefore, all the more significant.

On the right, the protectionism of frightened industry, combined with a certain jingoistic nationalism inherited from the First World War, formed the basis of the attitude of the opponents of the Treaty, while the arguments of those in favor were inspired by anti-communism and—among some of the young people—a desire for real, living and federalist order.[9] The independents, in fact, were just as divided as the socialists: the unfavorable view taken by several military authorities—Marshals Juin and Weygand—was to have a considerable influence on their attitudes.[10]

Unfortunately, as the debate continued, it grew increasingly embittered, an impassioned controversy dividing people into opposing factions, even members of the same family—calling to mind the Dreyfus affair. This time, however, party labels became less and less relevant: at meetings on the European movement, communists and nationalists could be seen sharing the same platform, similarly "clericals" and "seculars," and "conservatives" and "progressives."

The last act was deplorable, even in the eyes of many opponents of the Plan. Several months before 30 August, the Laniel government finally lost power, mainly through its own weakness. On 7 May, the fortress of Dien Bien Phu had fallen, and while the Geneva Peace Conference dragged on, the military situation in the Red River Delta was rapidly deteriorating. In desperation, the National Assembly voted Pierre Mendès-France into power; he promised to put an end to the hopeless conflict, and for several weeks enjoyed enormous prestige.

What were his views on the European army? It was difficult to know precisely. Undoubtedly, his basic inclinations led him to seek pacifist and federal solutions, as did his economic foresight. Like Herriot, he had, several years earlier, come out in favor of the European Movement. In 1930 he had written a book (published by Valois), the technical title of which, *La Banque internationale: Contribution à l'étude du problème des Etats-Unis d'Europe,* clearly indicated the nature of its political content.

In this work, written in his youth, and which he never disavowed, he made no secret of the federalist consequences of an international financial organization.[11] For example:

"It seems to me that it is in the adoption at the earliest possible moment of the European Customs Union, in the *rapprochement* of the various Western codes, in other words, in the creation of a United States of Europe, that effective remedies will be found to reassure the worried consciences of democrats and pacifists. . . ." "The creation of the International Bank necessitates the unification of Europe [and] calls for an even great urgency in implementing these New United States, which have been discussed so extensively but which have yet to be given any precise form."[12]

But although his basic inclinations were to lead him toward supranational solutions, other factors restrained him from going in this direction. He found it difficult to overcome his instinctive mistrust of this Germany against which he had fought with courage in the Free French air force. Moreover, the absence of Great Britain had a great effect upon him, and when he had to consider alternative solutions—we shall be returning to this question later —he quickly resigned himself to the loss of federalism by saying that now there was likely to be "less supranationality but more entente cordiale." Indeed, it is quite possible that the socialist deputy, Gérard Jacquet, was right in saying that basically "the EDC held little interest for him."[13] He was first and foremost a patriot and felt very deeply the humiliation and useless losses suffered by the French army in the debilitating rearguard action it was fighting in the Far East. Indochina took first priority for him. It has been claimed that Molotov took advantage of the disastrous military situation of the French in Asia to force him to abandon the idea of a European army, and it is possible that at the Geneva Conference, the Russian Minister may have proposed something along these lines. Certainly, the final Geneva agreement was more favorable to France than the Vietminh might reasonably have expected.[14] Yet what weight did these considerations carry in the decision?

Undoubtedly, Mendès-France, uneasy and undecided, turned reluctantly to the problem of the EDC. He realized it was necessary to find a solution one way or another but had no illusions about the opposition the Treaty would come up against in the National Assembly. Was it really worth fighting for such a badly drafted document, which was probably doomed to failure? Couldn't his neutrality enable him to continue in power at a time when France was in such urgent need of an intelligent and energetic government—his own?

He decided to renegotiate the EDC.

Did his proposals, which all tended to tone down the supranational elements, affect the basic issue? Gérard Jacquet does not think so. Others, such as the Dutch Foreign Minister[15] and Federal Chancellor Adenauer,[16] think they did. Paul-Henri Spaak, for his part, a born conciliator, did his utmost to find reasonable compromise solutions—without success. When the six ministers met in Brussels on 19 August, the die was cast, for the French Premier already carried in his pocket a final declaration, very carefully formulated, which made defeat inevitable.[17]

This breakdown of negotiations meant deadlock. By now four national parliaments had already ratified the Draft Treaty. It would have been virtually impossible to make them withdraw their votes by presenting them with a new Treaty which, in their eyes, would have been less satisfactory. Above all, Mendès-France was unable to inspire in his partners that sympathy, that understanding of his domestic problems so indispensable in order to reach agreement. An "emotional" personality such as his can arouse either a spontaneous desire to meet him halfway and support him or, on the other hand, a feeling of irritation. It was the latter reaction which he aroused, and in such a delicate situation these emotional feelings play an important, even a decisive, part in negotiations. The desire to force his partners to have confidence in him or, at least, to make them bear the responsibility for the setback ended in their categorical refusal. Spaak describes the meeting as follows:

> During the Brussels conference, he suffered continuously from complexes vis-à-vis his partners, which made his task more complicated and his actions less effective. He was convinced that they did not like him, that they did not have confidence in him, that they considered him as an intruder, that he was there in the role of a defendant before his partial judges.
>
> During these sessions, he was forever doodling on the paper lying on the table in front of him. A lot of people have this mania. Some draw flowers, others animals, others women. He was always drawing huge, thick walls, prison walls. He really thought, I am sure, that he was being persecuted. He persuaded people in France to believe that this was the case. I shall have no difficulty in proving that nothing was further from the truth.[18]

In the early hours of the morning, when the six ministers left Spaak's office, nothing had been agreed—and in reply to a journalist who asked what captions he should write under the photograph, Adenauer replied, "Six Tired Europeans."

Notes:

[1] Herbert Lüthy, *La France à l'heure de son clocher* (Paris: Calmann-Lévy, 1955).

[2] François Fontaine, *La Nation Frein* (Paris: Julliard, 1956), pp. 70–71.

[3] Quoted by Guy de Carmoy, *Fortune de l'Europe* (Paris: Domat Montchrestien, 1953), p. 297.

[4] Schuman realized this. In the *Samedi Soir* of 19 March 1953, he wrote an article entitled "Savoir se décider," from which the following is quoted: ". . . The moment has come to confront the innumerable distortions which continue to be circulated. . . . Supporters of the Treaty must stop giving the impression that they are already resigned to failure. We must put an end to this 'strange war' in which the supporters of the Treaty hide themselves away and leave all the initiative to their opponents."

[5] These figures and those which follow can be found in the article "L'Opinion publique devant la C.E.D.," by Alain Girard and Jean Stoetzel, in Raymond Aron and Daniel Lerner, *La Querelle de la C.E.D.* (Paris: Armand Colin, 1956), pp. 127ff.

[6] Léo Hamon, who later became a left-wing Gaullist, was one of them.

[7] Erlind Bjöl, *La France devant l'Europe; European politics in the Fourth Republic* (Copenhagen: Munksgaard, 1966), p. 154. The author considers that, on this occasion, the Socialist policy was "a hotchpotch of contradictions."

[8] *Ibid.*, p. 170.

[9] Cf. on this subject the very idealized picture of the right drawn by Jean Jaélic, *La Droite, cette inconnue* (Paris: Les Sept Couleurs, 1963): "Yes, for a Frenchman today, our real fatherland is Europe. . . . To sum up: nationalism and internationalism are on the Left; patriotism is on the Right. The French nation is on the Left as is, in practice, the international of the United Nations; the European fatherland is on the Right." (Pp. 254 and 260.)

[10] On this subject, as on many others and especially the ECSC, see Ernst B. Haas, *The Uniting of Europe, Political, Social and Economic Forces 1950–1957* (London: Stevens, 1958).

[11] He also returned to a clearly pro-European position in his small book, *La République moderne* (Paris: N.R.F., 1963).

[12] Quoted by Erling Bjöl, *op. cit.*, p. 176.

[13] Interview quoted in *ibid.*, p. 359.

[14] For example, Stanley Karlow: "Peace Table Betrayals Haunt Hanoi," *International Herald Tribune*, 7 May 1968.

[15] Cf. the memoirs of the latter, J. W. Beyen, *Het Spel en de Knikkers* (Rotterdam: A. Donker, 1968).

[16] Konrad Adenauer, *op. cit.*, p. 255: "I wondered what M. Mendès-France was really after. I couldn't imagine he believed his proposals were acceptable. I began to wonder whether his aim was to bring about the collapse of the E.D.C. But not daring to announce his refusal openly, he used the expedient

of these unacceptable amendments. In so doing, he seemed to want to make those who had rejected his offer responsible for the failure."

[17] This is what Paul-Henri Spaak asserts in his memoirs.

[18] Paul-Henri Spaak, *Combats inachevés: I. De l'Indépendance à l'alliance* (Paris: Fayard, 1969), p. 274.

POSITIVE INTEGRATION AND NEGATIVE INTEGRATION: SOME PROBLEMS OF ECONOMIC UNION IN THE EEC
BY JOHN PINDER

Most politicians voting in favor of the Treaties of Rome did so in the belief that they were accepting economic sacrifices in return for political gains. John Pinder reviews the economic arguments in favor of customs unions, and identifies the main areas in which progress had been made toward economic union in EEC by 1968. He concludes that future economic gains will require a recovery of the momentum toward political union. This chapter originally appeared as an article in the March 1968 issue of The World Today *(Vol. 24, pp. 88–110), the monthly journal published by the Royal Institute of International Affairs, London. It is reprinted here by permission of the journal and the author.*[1]

1 / DEFINITION OF ECONOMIC INTEGRATION

When we talk about economic integration in Europe, the intelligent listener usually assumes that we are talking about the European Economic Community and perhaps its two sister Communities, and the intelligent listener is usually right. But when we try to analyse the problems of integration with some precision, we shall find ourselves in trouble unless we have a more precise definition. The most important problems are largely uncharted; but a precise definition at least removes an unnecessary source of difficulty.

According to the *Concise Oxford English Dictionary*, integration is the combination of parts into a whole, and union is a whole resulting from the combination of parts or members. Thus integration is the process of reaching the state of union. It seems better to distinguish between union and integration in this way, rather than to sow a seed of confusion in the discussion by defining integration as meaning both the process and the state, as Balassa does.[2]

The important choice now lies in the definition of union: in other words, in deciding when a combination of economic parts or members, in this case national economies, is to be regarded as a whole. Balassa says that a state of economic union has been reached when there is not only free movement of products and factors of production between a group of countries, but also "some degree of harmonization of national economic policies in order to remove discrimination that was due to disparities in these policies."

It often happens that the whole character of an argument is governed by the definitions of the key words that are used, and in my view there is a danger that the problems of economic integration in the European Communities will be misunderstood if discussion is based on this definition of economic union. As I will argue later, once the member countries of the Community have removed from the economic transactions between their citizens most of the discrimination that was formerly caused by the fact that those citizens were subject to different national laws and regulations, it is essential for those countries to go farther. If they are to deal with the problems that result from the freedom of transactions between their citizens, and to make the most of the opportunities for increasing welfare that are offered by the larger market, they must co-ordinate their national policies and form common policies in many ways that go beyond the mere removal of discrimination. Balassa recognizes that this may be desired, and therefore goes on to define "total economic integration" which "presupposes the unification of monetary, fiscal, social and countercyclical policies and requires the setting-up of a supranational authority whose decisions are binding for the member states."[3] But there are two main objections to Balassa's definitions.

First, economic union is the term used, in contemporary discussions in the Community, for the economic destination of the EEC; and if economic union is defined as the removal of discrimination, it may be implicitly assumed that this represents the limit of the process of integration in the Community. According to what may be called "free trade ideology" this would indeed be the best result. But I do not think that it is a sensible result in an age when economic policies are required to stabilize both prices and balances of payments, to secure both full employment and rapid economic growth, and to aim at a number of other objectives designed to maximize welfare; and in circumstances where the removal of instruments for acting unilaterally on the balance of payments reduces the possibility for the government of each member country to attain these objectives by means of its own policies.

The second objection to Balassa's definitions is that "total economic integration" sounds as if the economy of the union is going to become a replica of an existing national economy (and the word total implies a tightly centralized one, at that), with the national governments being reduced, for economic purposes, to the role of, say, a state government in the United States. This may eventually happen. But one of the most interesting questions that can be asked about economic integration, and indeed about political integration, is whether it does have to go as far as that, or whether there is an intermediate position between national independence and the role of the state in the American federal system, where the member countries of a union can act jointly with enough decision to satisfy their main objectives. If this is found to be possible, the pattern of regional organization in existing nation-states might move in the direction shown by the experience of the Community, not the other way about. It would be a great pity if the definition of economic integration and economic union made this question more difficult to ask.

I will therefore define economic integration as both the removal of discrimination, as between the economic agents of the member countries, and the formation and application of co-ordinated and common policies on a sufficient scale to ensure that major economic and welfare objectives are fulfilled. It follows that economic union is a state in which discrimination has been largely removed, and co-ordinated and common policies have been and are being applied on a sufficient scale.

For a clear discussion about the European Communities, it is necessary further to have a word for the removal of discrimination by itself, without the other elements of economic integration. Here I will use two terms that have been used by Tinbergen, although again it seems necessary to change his definitions so as to make the terms as useful as possible, in the light of the experience of the Community as it has evolved.[4] The terms are negative integration and positive integration, and I will use negative integration for that part of economic integration that consists of the removal of discrimination, and positive integration as the formation and application of co-ordinated and common policies in order to fulfil economic and welfare objectives other than the removal of discrimination.

Negative and positive integration together comprise economic integration, whose end is economic union. The end of negative integration unaccompanied by positive integration may be called a common market, although it may be objected that the Rome Treaty, and still more current usage, employs the term common market ambiguously, sometimes including and sometimes excluding some of the fruits of positive integration. I know of no case where it has been proposed to unite a group of countries by means of positive integration without negative integration. But this is by no means inconceivable, nor indeed would the result have to be very different from a national economy with a regional policy that discriminates powerfully in favour of that nation's less-favoured regions. This is, admittedly, normally done with instruments such as tax allowances, subsidies, cheap loans, low transport rates, government buying policies, etc., and not by means of import and exchange controls on transactions between the region and the rest of the country. The Rome Treaty foresees that member governments will wish to pursue such policies for their development regions, and expressly allows them to be pursued, subject to the Commission's agreement that the aid, or discrimination in favour of the region, is not excessive. To this extent the EEC, like many national economies, intentionally falls short of complete negative integration. It is thus possible that positive integration will be undertaken by a group of countries without complete negative integration, and this may indeed, in an age when regional policies are prevalent, become the normal form of economic integration. Whether the discrimination in favour of regions will always be confined to "non-tariff barriers," or whether regional import and exchange controls might sometimes be found to be a useful device, is another question, that need not be dealt with here.

For what Balassa calls an "all-out liberalist,"[5] a common market and an economic union are the same thing, because for him negative integration constitutes common policies on a sufficient scale to ensure that major economic and welfare objectives are fulfilled. For me, a common market is a far lesser thing than an economic union, and without economic union will prove to be unviable.

2 / TRADE CREATION AND TRADE DIVERSION: THE STATIC EFFECTS OF CUSTOMS UNIONS

The movement towards economic integration in the last two decades has evoked a considerable quantity of economic literature, much of which has been concerned with the immediate effects on trade and hence on welfare of the establishment of a free trade area or a customs union. This part of the literature has, on the whole, been based on the analytical apparatus bequeathed to us by the classical economists and thus on static equilibrium assumptions, that is, on the assumptions that resources, including the stock of capital, are given, and that if the existing equilibrium is upset by any change, for example by the removal of a tariff, forces will come into play that will cause it to be replaced by a new equilibrium position.

The first landmark for the post-war debates on customs unions and free trade areas was Viner's famous work.[6] Viner challenged the assumption, hitherto accepted by liberal economists, that any customs union, being a step in the direction of free trade, would increase the sum total of welfare in the world. As is well known, he divided the changes in trade that would result from a customs union into trade creation, where new trade between members of the customs union would replace higher-cost production in the importing member, and trade diversion, where existing imports from a non-member would be replaced by imports from a member. The trade creation would cause an increase in welfare because higher-cost production would be replaced by lower-cost; the diversion would reduce welfare because the old imports from a non-member were, since they had been bought by the importing country when the same tariff had faced the member and the non-member, clearly lower-cost than the new imports which replaced them because of the tariff preference. Thus any proposal for a customs union should be examined to discover how much trade creation and how much trade diversion there would be, before any judgement could be formed as to whether welfare would be enlarged or reduced.

After Viner had shown that the changes in trade caused by the establishment of a customs union could be the subject of an interesting analysis, other economists pursued his line of thought and, from Viner's small beginnings, evolved a theory of customs unions of considerable refinement. Meade in particular lent his mind to this exercise.[7] He showed that, in order to calculate the changes in trade that would follow directly from the mutual reduction of tariffs on the trade between a group of countries, it would be necessary to take account of a number of factors including the initial heights of the tariffs and the sizes of the cuts (assuming a preferential area was possible as well as a free trade area or customs union), the competitiveness or complementarity of the economies taking part, the elasticities of demand and supply, the change in the amount of consumer surplus, the effect on the terms of trade, and the relative incomes of those from whom and in favour of whom trade was diverted. He concluded that the gains/losses in total welfare would be greatest/least in proportion as the tariffs to be reduced were initially higher/lower; the cuts in them were deeper/shallower; the member economies were the more competitive/complementary; the member countries' mutual trade was a higher/lower proportion of their total trade and a higher/lower proportion of total world trade in the products traded between the members; the greater/less the scope for economies of scale in the industries that gain from trade creation; and the more/less all-embracing the union, in terms of both countries and products.[8]

This theory as it has been developed by Meade and others is fairly tough fare and serves to sharpen the intellectual teeth. It is therefore a good instrument of education. But there are two major reasons why it is not a useful guide for practical policy: the "static" effects of trade creation and trade diversion are probably much less important than the "dynamic" effects on economic growth via influences on competition, investment and the balance of payments; and customs unions tend to be set up for "political" reasons rather than because of econometricians' forecasts of changes in trade, from which it follows that economic analysis would be more fruitfully focused on the implication for economic policy of the existence of customs unions than on the justification of custom unions in terms of forecast changes in the flows of trade.

3 / THE DYNAMIC EFFECTS OF FREE TRADE

During the last decade the view has gained ground that the static analysis indicated by Viner's approach is in any case relatively unimportant,[9] even if this approach can be subjected to an elegant theoretical analysis and to quantitative forecasts of greater or lesser plausibility. Lipsey, reviewing the estimates made by Verdoorn,[10] and by Johnson[11] on the basis of the forecasts made by the Economist Intelligence Unit,[12] as well as making his own "common sense check" based on feasible savings in costs due to the freeing of trade, accepted that the best estimates gave "figures of the net gain from trade amounting to something less than 1 per cent of the national income."[13]

The reason for this small order of magnitude is that the "static gain" to welfare due to increases in trade is equal, not to the increment in trade itself, but to that increment multiplied by the reduction in cost due to changes in the source of production (Johnson based his estimates on the percentage of the tariffs that would be removed). Thus large forecasts of trade increases, such as those made by the Economist Intelligence Unit for a wide European free trade area or by Stamp and Cowie[14] for a free trade area comprising Britain, Canada and the United States (which they called NAFTA), turn out to imply very small, once-for-all increases in GNP. It clearly needs only a small dynamic effect on the rate of growth of GNP, say an increment of 0.1 per cent a year compound for twenty years, to far outweigh effects of this order of magnitude due to direct trade creation and trade diversion.

It can of course be argued that gains from trade creation or trade diversion will themselves have a very important dynamic effect if, for example, they replace a balance-of-payments deficit by a surplus and thus remove the external constraint from an economy whose growth is checked by that constraint, or conversely, if they cause or intensify an external deficit that checks growth. Thus a net gain of $550–$650 million such as Stamp and Cowie forecast for Britain within a NAFTA might, by solving the balance-of-payments problem, allow the British economy a substantially faster rate of growth; or a £600 million worsening of the UK deficit, forecast by *The Times* "Business News"[15] if Britain were to join the European Communities, could prevent such growth as the British economy might otherwise achieve. But these once-for-all trade effects can be achieved/countered, according as they are favourable/unfavourable, by once-for-all measures such as devaluation (which in the case of the devaluation of November 1967 was forecast to improve the balance of payments by a still larger amount); and the dynamic effects of customs unions on, for example, investment remain of very much greater potential importance than the effects through the immediate impact on trade. An act of policy such as the creation of a free trade area, customs union or economic union, which is likely to take some years to establish and then to have over a long period profound economic and perhaps political effects going far beyond the immediate impact on the balance of payments, would indeed be a strange instrument to use in order to rectify a current payments deficit.

The work that has been done so far on the economies of scale and the extent to which they can be derived in markets of various size has been reviewed by Balassa[16] and by Swann and McLachlan.[17] They conclude that the gains from a market larger than that of the UK could be significant. The most interesting analysis of the possible gains from production for a wider market remains, however, that of Scitovsky,[18] who makes some points that appear to be important, particularly in relation to Britain's circumstances, but that do not seem to have been further developed theoretically, let alone tested by empirical research.

Scitovsky suggests that the crucial factor in a firm's decision whether to invest in new and optimum plant is whether the firm will (expect to?) be able to increase sales by the amount that such plant will produce. This depends on the annual increment in the total market, on the market share of the firm in question, on the speed and extent to which customers will switch their allegiance towards a cheaper or better product and on the energy with which the firm will seek to encroach on its competitors' market shares: in fact on the size of the market, its expected rate of growth, the size of firm and the competitiveness of consumers' and producers' behaviour. In Britain's case, the change in these factors resulting from membership of the EEC (or of a NAFTA) would be such as to make British firms a great deal more prone to invest in optimum equipment. The size of market to which the manufacturer of the average product would be confident of having free access would be greatly increased. Even if the growth performance in the EEC is not what it was, the expectation would still probably, and reasonably enough, be that the rate of growth of the total market will continue to be faster and certainly less liable to sudden interruptions in the EEC (or in the USA) than in Britain on its own. The customers in Britain, whether consumers or those who purchase on behalf of firms, are thought to be more conservative and slower than those on the continent (or in the USA) to switch their suppliers. And many British businessmen seem to have been inclined to base their attitudes to their competitors' markets on those of a country gentleman towards his neighbour's property: poaching has been widely held to break the rules of the game. This ethic seems less widespread on the continent and in America; and more important, businessmen are less likely to have such fine feelings for the welfare of their competitors where these are industrialists from another country, rather than coming from their own country and thus more likely to be known personally.

It is possible that these factors would have a great effect on the investment decisions of firms whose environment has hitherto been the relatively small, slow-growing and uncompetitive British market. Scitovsky's analysis certainly failed to take account of the greater opportunity for a firm to invest in optimum plant when it is possible for the firm to write off existing plant (the capacity of the plant to be written off being added to the expected increments to sales); but even so the opportunities for investment in optimum plant would surely be greatly increased. The same argument applies to modernization through reorganized production, for example, as part of a productivity bargain, because the gains would be larger and more certain and would thus more readily outweigh the inconvenience of change.

Thus the dynamic gains due to considerations of "scale" and the "climate of competition" seem likely to be far more important than the static gains or losses due to trade creation and trade diversion, at least for a country the size of Britain and in the economic circumstances a more doubtful element as far as Britain is concerned, however, particularly in relation to the NAFTA proposal.

The protection of industries that are weak because they are new has long been justified by the infant-industry exception to the classical free trade theory. More recently this exception has been generalized so as to apply to the whole of industry in a less-developed economy. But the idea that the dynamic effects of free trade may be such as to wither the growth of a weaker economy has been little supported by economic theory, chiefly no doubt because the theory of growth is still underdeveloped in relation to equilibrium theory, and because growth theory, such as it is, has concentrated on the problems of growth within a single national economy, and without much attention, either, to the problems of regions within a national economy, which are analogous to the problems of growth and balance of payments of the member countries of a free trade area, customs union or economic union. But Prebisch has provided some theoretical justifications of the practice of protection of underdeveloped countries;[19] and Streeten has discussed the problem with particular reference to economic integration in Europe.[20]

The pessimistic view of the impact on a weaker economy (southern Ireland, southern Italy) of free trade with a more dynamic economy (England, northern Italy) is based on the following type of argument. According to the classical equilibrium theory, the weaker area should export those goods in which it has a comparative advantage and, if the exchange rate is such as to allow equilibrium in its balance of payments, the weaker area will have a comparative advantage in enough products. If further movements are possible moreover, capital will flow there to take advantage of the cheap labour.

According to the pessimistic view, however, the trade of the weaker area with the dynamic area will always be running into deficit because the dynamic one will always be developing new and better products or lower-cost methods of production, so as to undermine the comparative advantage of the weaker area at the existing exchange rate. The weaker area therefore has the alternative of continually devaluing its currency or depressing its wages, or reducing its area income by deflating. If the weaker area is part of the same national economy or economic union its case is even worse, because it probably cannot devalue; capital will flow to the dynamic region where, even if wages are higher, the economic and social infrastructure is better and the business environment is such as to lead people to expect higher profits; and the enterprising people will move to the dynamic area, thus continually draining the weaker area of its energy and talent.

This argument may or may not be correct. But the important thing to realize is that, at the present state of the theory and of the evidence on this subject, it is impossible to know whether, or in what circumstances, the argument is correct or not. The classical free trade theory, beautiful though it is, does not deal with this problem and therefore neither confirms or disproves it; the evidence of southern Ireland and southern Italy is not altogether supported by the evidence of the southern states of the USA, which for a number of years did manage to show a faster growth than that for the United States as a whole. One still has to form a judgement as to whether the weak economy suffers a cumulative loss in competition with the dynamic, and if so what exactly is a weak economy and what is a dynamic one.

My own judgement is that the prolonged existence of regional problems in many countries shows that the pessimistic view of the effect of free movement of products and, even more, of factors between a weak economy and a dynamic economy is in certain (not rare) circumstances, or with certain (not very restricted) definitions of weak and dynamic, the correct view; and that for this purpose, the attributes of a weak/dynamic economy are likely to include a low/high income per head, a low/high degree of capital-intensiveness and R and D-intensiveness, and a low/high degree of competitive dynamism (a question-begging attribute, but one that seems to be recognizable if one moves from Tokyo to Bombay). Specifically, I would be pessimistic about the prospects for Britain in a NAFTA *à la* Stamp and Cowie comprising Britain, Canada and the United States, but not about the prospects of a Britain in the European Community.

It may be said that this is no better than guesswork, and that is indeed true. But it is worth repeating that, if there are any dynamic effects of free trade, whether of the kind examined by Scitovsky (investments, etc.) or by Streeten (cumulative balance-of-payments effects), they are likely to be much more important than the static effects of immediate trade creation and trade diversion. As so often, one has to use one's judgment about the more important factor; and it would be foolish to attach excessive weight to the less important, just because it is more readily subject to elaborate theoretical or numerical treatment.

4 / THE POLITICAL MOTIVES FOR ESTABLISHING FREE TRADE SYSTEMS OR ECONOMIC UNIONS

As I suggested earlier, the motives for establishing or joining economic groupings such as free trade areas, customs unions or economic unions usually have more to do with political orientation than with calculations of economic gain. This was certainly the case with the European Communities; and it was also the case with the British application to join the Communities, announced in May 1967, for when the application was made the official forecasts of the net effect on British trade and the British balance of payments had been very discouraging. It is true that the dynamic and longer-term effects were in both cases believed to be beneficial; but these beliefs, depending more on subjective judgements than on scientific deduction, spring from the same part of the mind as the political orientations, and it should not be a cause for surprise that, for most economists, long-term economic judgement and political orientation point in the same direction, nor is there any evidence that the economic judgement usually precedes the political orientation.

Meade himself, after devoting a considerable intellectual effort to the refining of the theory of trade creation and trade diversion, wrote that, if he were a citizen of a Benelux country, he knew very well that he would be "an ardent proponent and supporter of the building of Benelux even if a careful and unbiassed application of criteria which I have just enumerated suggested that its formation was more likely to reduce rather than to raise economic welfare in the rather narrow sense in which I have been using the term," because "larger social and political units are likely to be more viable and self-reliant politically and strategically" and "there is a need for greater integration of the countries of the free world."[21]

Surely we need no further encouragement to turn from the subject of the economic pros and cons of establishing or joining customs unions, which has occupied so much of economists' attention to date, to that of the problems that arise for economic policy when a customs union is in fact created.

5 / POLICIES IN THE EUROPEAN COMMUNITIES: THE BIAS AGAINST ECONOMIC UNION

We can now draw upon ten years' experience of the creation of a customs union and of moves towards economic union consisting of a group of large and advanced Western countries, and we can therefore take a significant step away from pure speculation and towards the analysis of evidence, although as we shall see the most interesting and important questions remain unanswered by the experience so far.

It is useful to consider two main aspects of the problems of the

European Community and of the policies that have been or could be designed by the Community to deal with the problems.

The problems can be divided into those that arise in the process of trying to eliminate discrimination between the economic agents in the different member states (the problems of negative integration, or of establishing a common market, as defined earlier) and those that arise in a collective attempt by the member countries to maximize welfare in the customs union (the problems of positive integration, or of establishing an economic union).

The policies can be divided into those that have a strong chance of being implemented (strong political motives, strong provision in the Treaty and/or in the Community's institutional procedures) and those that have a weak chance.

There is a one-sided relationship between these two dichotomies which is very important in understanding what has been achieved so far in the Communities and what problems are likely to arise in the future. This is that the policies which have a strong chance of being implemented are those that deal with negative integration, while those with a weaker chance are those concerned with positive integration. "Free trade ideology" is firmly built into the system, but the "planning ethic" is no more than a possibility for the future. There are four main reasons for this.

First, the one thing on which almost everyone concerned with the foundation of the Communities was agreed was that they were inaugurating a new deal for Europe in which war between the member countries would become unthinkable, and that they should therefore as far as possible cease to treat the citizens of other members as foreigners by discriminating against them. Non-discrimination has become a deep-rooted reflex among those who run the Communities.

Second, it is not difficult to provide in a treaty for the removal of discrimination, which is relatively simple to define and to enforce. But it is much harder to ensure by means of a treaty that an effective common policy will be formed; for a policy might take any one of a thousand forms, and it will usually be hard to attribute to any individual or government responsibility for failure to define a common policy, and still more for failure to define an effective one. In short, a treaty can more easily make effective the "thou shalt not" commandments than the "thou shalt" ones.

Third, the neo-liberals who were until recently in sole control of the German government adhered to an economic ideology that stressed free trade and rather strictly circumscribed the role of economic policy. Dr. Erhard in particular was opposed to the idea that Brussels should become a policy-making power house. Given the importance of Germany in the Community, this placed a severe limit on the extent of common policy-making.

Fourth, General de Gaulle, who is also at present an important element in the Community, adheres to a political ideology that violently rejects the idea of any authority above or outside the nation-state, and the French government has therefore ferociously resisted the institutional procedures by which common or co-ordinated policies on the complex issues of positive integration are likely to be brought about. More passively, there is a natural tendency for other national bureaucracies and government machines to resist any loss of their power of unilateral decision and action, which is inevitably implied in an effective procedure for taking decisions in common.

Apart from General de Gaulle, who was in temporary retirement when the Rome Treaty establishing the EEC was negotiated and signed, all these factors influenced the content of the Rome Treaty, which is therefore in its detail strongly biased in the direction of negative integration and away from positive integration. This is illustrated in Article 3 of the Treaty, which outlines the activities of the Community, as well as in later articles where some details are filled in. Thus, Article 3 speaks of "the elimination, as between member states, of customs duties and of quantitative restrictions . . . as well as of other measures with equivalent effect"; and "the establishment of a common customs tariff": very precise objectives, which are specified in detail in later articles. Then there is "the abolition as between member states, of the obstacles to the free movement of persons, services, and capital" and "the establishment of a system ensuring that competition shall not be distorted in the Common Market": equally unequivocal objectives of negative integration, whose implementation is however more complicated than is the establishment of the customs union, and is therefore less precisely provided for later in the Treaty.

Article 3 also specifies a common commercial policy, a common agricultural policy and a common transport policy; these sound definite enough, but, as has already been noted, it is much easier for the member governments to default on their obligation to form an undefined common policy than it is for them to evade their promises to remove discrimination and distortions.

When Article 3 comes to such crucial elements of positive integration as economic policies and balance-of-payments problems it becomes extremely vague and permissive instead of definite and mandatory. It merely writes of "the application of procedures which shall make it possible to co-ordinate the economic policies of Member States and to remedy disequilibria in their balances of payments." In the body of the Treaty there is only one article, and a pretty feeble one at that, dealing with "policy relating to economic trends," and six articles dealing with balance-of-payments problems, compared with twenty-nine on the establishment of the customs union.

The remaining items listed in Article 3 are the "approximation" of laws, which concerns mainly the removal of discrimination and distortions; the creation of the Social Fund and the Investment Bank, which are certainly elements of economic union but which, with their present resources, can have only a small influence; and the association of overseas countries and territories.

Article 3 accurately reflects the emphasis of the Treaty on the removal of discrimination and distortions, i.e., on negative integration and the consequent establishment of a common market.

The next article refers to the Community's institutions, Assembly, Council, Commission, and Court, which constitute the other main concrete achievement of the Treaty itself. As will be seen from the following section, however, the only other big steps towards the economic union of the member countries have resulted from the political bargain between France and Germany over the agricultural policy and the Kennedy Round.

6 / POLICIES IN THE EUROPEAN COMMUNITIES: THE FIVE MAJOR ACHIEVEMENTS

The first great policy achievement of the European Community has, of course, been the establishment of the customs union. The programme for this was laid down in detail in the Rome Treaty, and by 1 July 1968 it was virtually completed, sooner than was originally planned.

The Community's second major policy achievement has been the creation of the agricultural common market. Free trade is harder to establish for products in relation to which the member countries have managed markets because the cheaper product is as likely to be the more-subsidized as it is to be the lower-cost, and member countries would rightly refuse to accept the unfair competition represented by a flood of imports of some foodstuffs from another member country that were cheaper than the domestic product solely because they were more subsidized by the other member country's government. It follows that the only alternatives are to stop managing the markets for such products or to manage them in common. The Community chose the latter course with respect to agricultural products, and it was clear from the amount of attention given in the Rome Treaty to the agricultural policy that a high priority was attached to it.

The reason for this was simple. French industry was weak in relation to German industry, but French agriculture, based on very favourable natural conditions, was in a strong competitive position, with excellent prospects for the future. Economically, the European Community was for France a bargain in which a risk was taken for French industry in exchange for a great and certain gain for French agriculture. If this bargain had not been kept, General de Gaulle would have broken the Community by withdrawing France from it. The Germans as well as the other members knew this, and therefore agreed, after long, difficult and repeated sessions in the Council of Ministers, to a common agricultural policy, which consists of a system for the fixing of prices on a common Community basis, and for supporting these price levels notably with the help of import levies and subsidies to producers.[22] The achievement of this most thorny task was a notable triumph for the Community system in general and the Commission in particular. It is probably true to say that never before had an international organization succeeded in shaping a common policy with respect to which such sensitive national interests were so deeply involved.

Notable though the achievement was, however, its importance as a contribution to positive integration should not be exaggerated. In effect the "policy" has so far almost entirely centred on the fixing of a common price (and an uneconomically high one at that), which is the only way of removing discrimination as between the member states: the system has been called "merely a complicated kind of customs union." The "guidance" part of the guidance and guarantee fund (FEOGA), which was originally fixed at £100 million a year, provides a basis of a positive policy aimed at the structural improvement of agriculture and of the predominantly agricultural regions of the Community. But the reaction of the Council of Ministers was that only half of this amount should be spent jointly, and that the other half should be returned to the national governments to be spent in their own agricultural programmes.[23]

In the other main managed-market sectors, energy and transport, the Community has made relatively little progress towards an effective common policy. A co-ordinated or common policy for the main types of energy, hampered hitherto by the division of responsibility between the three separate communities, is still only at an embryonic stage. Even in the several energy markets the experience has been disappointing. The European Coal and Steel Community successfully inaugurated free trade in coal during the mid-1950's, when there was a sellers' market; but since the coal mines have been in difficulty the national governments have largely taken responsibility for defending their interests and the role of the Community's common policy has been minimized. Euratom, too, got off to a good start, with a very active research programme initiated at a time when it was expected that a large output of nuclear power would be wanted fairly quickly. Since then, however, the timetable for nuclear power generation has been put back and member governments, with the French government in the lead, have stressed their national programmes at the expense of Euratom. The Euratom budget is under severe pressure, and agreement on a research programme is proving very difficult.

In the field of transport, there has been some progress with the removal of discrimination, but a common policy for the development of the Community's transport is still a distant and shadowy prospect, while a pricing policy, based on a "fork" of maximum and minimum rates, is still in its early stages.

When the ECSC was established there was provision for a managed market in steel at times of severe under- or over-production, to be based likewise on a fork of maximum and minimum prices. But although there has been critical over-production, particularly in 1963–64, the High Authority of the ECSC has been politically too weak in relation to the member governments to make use of these possibilities, and the only effective action it could take was to get the member states to increase their protection against imports (and this was done by a constitutional sleight of hand, showing how the institutional procedures can affect the outcome even when the member governments are not willing to co-operate in framing a common policy).[24]

The experience of the Community is, then, that with respect to managed markets a common policy that is at all effective has been formed and applied only where there was a political motive powerful enough to over-ride the very tough national interests that exist in these sectors; and even where, as in agriculture, an effective common policy has been formed, it has tended to be based on the sum of the member countries' protectionisms rather than on a rational conception of the welfare of the Community as a whole. It must be added that this weakness in forming policies of positive integration has been due, to an extent that we cannot measure but may suppose to have been considerable, to the presence of General de Gaulle at the head of the French government during the whole period of the EEC's existence, which has added an element of abnormal activism to the passive resistance to the reduction of their national powers that may be expected from most national governments most of the time.

The third major policy achievement of the Community has been the successful negotiation of the Kennedy Round. This was partly thanks to the bargain between France and Germany, whereby France got the common agricultural policy while Germany got satisfaction for its industrial interests, who were very keen on freer trade. To some extent, perhaps, the common external tariff is the Community's international status symbol, and the ability to negotiate a major tariff agreement was felt to be a test of its international standing. Whatever the reasons, however, the conclusion of the Kennedy Round remains as a massive exception to the theory that the Community as it stands is unable to pursue policies of positive integration.

Some other aspects of the Community's performance in its attempts to evolve a common commercial policy have been more reassuring to the proponents of this pessimistic theory. In relation to the less-developed countries in general and to Eastern Europe the Community has made no recognizable progress towards a common policy, although the Rome Treaty stipulates that a common commercial policy is to be formed by 1970. On the other hand, the treaties of association with Greece and Turkey were of some importance, and the system of association

for former colonies presents a not inconsiderable achievement.
But the original association arrangements for former colonies,
enshrined in the Treaty of Rome, were, like the agricultural
policy, accepted by other members as part of a bargain with
France. The French government was in a strong position because
France was essential to the creation of the Community (Germany
plus the other four being too unbalanced a group to be politically viable); and late in the negotiations on the Treaty the
French insisted on the inclusion of the association system, which
the others accepted in order to get France to sign. This association was formally renewed in the Yaoundé Convention, when a
certain reduction in preferences was traded for a certain increase
in aid, at the same time as the system was endowed with institutions that recognize the sovereign status that almost all the associated countries had by then acquired. The lessons of this
association system, which may be regarded as a case of positive
integration, are that it came into existence because of a strong
manifestation of political will on the part of France (securing
the agreement of the others by threatening that there would be no
Community if they failed to agree), and that it then became a
fairly stable factor in the Community system.[25]

The fourth major policy achievement has been the cartel
policy. This started with the ECSC, where the High Authority
was given sharp teeth to prevent the formation of concentrations
of economic power caused by mergers of big steel companies.
Recently, however, the need for larger units has been accepted,
and mergers that would formerly have been prevented are being
allowed. The EEC in turn adopted a system of cartel policy that
gives the Commission considerable power to decide what kind of
cartel agreements affecting intra-Community trade shall be
allowed, subject to appeal to the European Court of Justice.
Although the Commission does not yet seem to have used this
power in such a way as to have any great influence on industry in
the Community, the system is an instrument of no small potential
importance.[26]

The cartel policy is, however, yet another aspect of negative integration, designed mainly to remove discrimination as between firms in the different member countries. The other side of this coin, representing an important aspect of positive integration, is industrial policy, which is still almost entirely at the stage of discussion rather than action at Community level. The European patent is fairly far advanced, but the plans for a European company and the unification of the capital markets are still at an earlier stage, and science policy (and *pro tanto* a technological community) is still almost virgin territory (apart from Euratom, which has now been raped).[27]

The fifth major achievement in Community policy is the agreement to adopt a uniform system of tax on value added (TVA). But here again the motive and implementation lie in the realm of negative integration: the TVA is to remove competitive distortions and, when the rate is made uniform in each country, to enable the member countries to abolish "fiscal frontiers" between them.[28] There is so far no element of positive integration: of the use of tax policy or tax revenue for ends other than the removal of discrimination, or of economic frontiers between the member states.[29]

The ECSC has its own taxing power in the form of a levy on the turnover of the enterprises in the coal and steel sectors, and this has been used for policies of positive integration such as the finance of research and of retraining, but the High Authority's political weakness has inhibited it from exploiting more than a fraction of the tax power given it by the Treaty establishing the ECSC, and it has operated on a correspondingly limited scale. The import levies on agricultural imports into the EEC are a major revenue-raiser, but this revenue is tied to the subsidization of agriculture, so that this turns out to be a distorted and unfair fiscal system, involving large transfers to the farmers and them alone from the consumers of imported foodstuffs and from them alone.

Thus the emphasis of the Community has been, in practice as much as in the letter of the Treaty establishing the EEC (which

is by far the most important of the three Communities), on negative rather than positive integration. The foregoing examination
of major policy successes and of a number of related failures confirms that the only successes that have encroached significantly on
the field of positive integration have been the common agricultural policy and the conclusion of the Kennedy Round, which
were the result of a major political bargain between France and
Germany; and to this may be added the Association of Overseas
States, the product of a similar bargain between France and the
Five.

There is no intention on my part to under-rate the Community's achievement in implementing enough measures of negative
integration to come within striking distance of the establishment
of a full common market, in which discrimination as between the
economic agents in the member countries has been virtually
removed, with respect to numerous non-tariff discriminations as
well as to import and exchange controls. This was a great task,
not only technically and economically but also because the frontiers have symbolized so much that was deplorable in the recent
history of Europe, politically and morally; and it is astonishing
that it has been so nearly accomplished. But I do intend to
emphasize that this achievement will be incomplete, and may
even be found to have created worse problems than it has solved,
unless equivalent progress is made in the field of positive integration, resulting in the creation of a full economic union.

7 / THE CASE FOR ECONOMIC UNION

There are a number of varieties of positive integration that
may be held to be necessary if a reasonable effort is to be made to
maximize welfare within a common market. Among these are
industrial policies, including the creation of large enough firms;
science and technology policies, including the financing of
research and development on the vast scale required in some
high-technology industries; policies towards investments in the
common market by firms originating in third countries; the

development of a modern transport network for the common market as a whole; rational policies in the sectors such as agriculture, energy, and transport, where goods or services traded between the members of the common market are subject to managed markets; policies of aid and assistance for development regions within the common market; common external policies relating to trade, aid and currencies, calculated to advance the interests of the common market as a whole and to create a satisfactory world economic environment. But here I will concentrate on one aspect of positive integration, which I believe may be found to be the most important: policies to deal with the member countries' balance-of-payments problems.

A country that is not a member of a common market or free trade system may use import controls, export subsidies, exchange controls or adjustments-of-exchange rates to help solve its balance-of-payments problems. These weapons are in principle denied to a member country of a common market. But such a country may well find itself in balance-of-payments trouble. Cost push or lax monetary or budgetary policies may push its costs above those of other countries, particularly of other member countries; the world market may evolve in such a way that the structure of its exports becomes ill-adapted to their growth at a satisfactory rate; its consumers' propensity to import may grow at a rate which its foreign exchange earnings cannot rival; or it may suffer from an endemic lack of dynamism of the type discussed earlier. If these things happen, the country has little alternative to deflation to rectify its deficit if it is not allowed to impose trade or exchange controls and if the common market lacks a common policy adequate to deal with the problem. Symmetrically, a country can suffer from balance-of-payments surpluses which are aggravated by its membership of a common market, but for simplicity the argument is confined to the problem of deficits.

Deflation may be an acceptable instrument if it rectified the trouble in a fairly short time, say inside a year. But suppose that a deflation is applied that is severe enough to stop economic growth and the deficit nevertheless persists; or the brakes are kept on sufficiently for payments to be in balance but growth is in consequence very slow for a long period. What can the country do, if it holds economic growth to be an important objective?

There are two broad alternatives. One is for the country to be allowed to contract out of the common market for a period by imposing trade or exchange controls as the French did in 1968, or to "distort the conditions of competition" by devaluing. These contingencies are allowed for in the Rome Treaty, but the Community system is severely shaken when they are applied; and the knowledge that their use is a major issue certainly stands in the way of a quick and efficient solution to the problem by means such as this.

The other alternative is for the common market to have joint policies, in the actual case operated by the institutions of the European Community, to deal with problems of this type. An examination of the way in which problems of inter-regional balance-of-payments and disparities in regional growth rates are dealt with in national economic systems may indicate the nature of the policies that would be required. It seems likely that these would include:

(a) *A large joint programme of aid for the growth of less-developed or ailing regions.* In countries where economic growth of the various regions is accepted as a major objective, aid for the improvement of infrastructure and for industrial development is an important arm of policy, which at the same time counters the structural deficits that such regions are likely to have in their balances of payments when they are enjoying economic growth. Aid provided jointly for such regions in a common market would make a big contribution to solving problems of balance of payments and inadequate growth in those member countries where such regions were important (or where indeed the whole country might constitute such a region or a group of such regions). The EEC can at present provide collective finance only at bankable rates of interest and through the modest resources of the Investment Bank. Without substantial powers to raise taxes and loans, the Community will not be able to perform these functions on the scale required to solve substantial balance-of-payments and growth problems of the member countries.

(b) *Development of transport facilities, and the granting of favourable transport rates*, that will encourage the economic growth of the less-favoured regions, and in particular of any region whose lack of dynamism is proving to be a drag on the balance of payments of a member country.

(c) *Unemployment and retraining assistance on a joint basis.* The flow of unemployment and retraining assistance within a national economy is an important equilibrator of both short-term and long-term regional deficits. The same would apply in a common market if unemployment assistance were collectively financed. The Social Fund of the EEC is empowered to finance half the cost of unemployment pay and of retraining for workers made redundant because of the establishment of the Common Market. If its scope were extended to cover unemployment and retraining in general it could become a substantial equilibrator, particularly of short-term deficits that are being met by deflation in the deficit country.

(d) *Fiscal and budgetary powers.* The strong budgetary role of a national government gives it powerful instruments for dealing with, among other things, problems of regional growth and balance of payments. In the European Community, fiscal powers could be used, not only as already indicated for regional development and for unemployment assistance, but also for purposes such as industrial policy, including the financing of R and D and structural improvements in declining industries, for social policy and for aid to less-developed countries, as well as for the agricultural subsidies that are the main object of expenditure in the EEC at present. Such budgetary powers give the official institutions scope for an influential role in the short-term capital market, in the course of financing leads and lags in expenditure and tax collection, as well as for applying regional policies in the form of tax remissions or in certain cases public purchasing arrangements that discriminate in favour of development regions.

(e) *The facilitating of labour migration.* Labour migration is one of the means of resolving the problem of disparities between regions in a national economy. Cultural differences will generally make this a less promising solution in a common market. It is, however, desirable at least that unnecessary barriers in the way of labour mobility should be removed, and the EEC, true to its practice of emphasizing negative integration, has done much in this direction.

(f) *A free flow of capital.* An efficient unified market for both long-term and short-term capital plays a major role in the inter-regional balance of payments of advanced countries. This role may be a dis-equilibrating one (cf. the argument about cumulative deficit problems for weak areas such as southern Italy), but equally it is hard to envisage an adequate equilibrating system that does not include a unified capital market. The EEC has made a good deal of progress in removing the legal and administrative barriers to the flow of capital between the member countries, but the capital market at community level remains relatively weak and ineffective, and a stronger system is essential for balance-of-payments reasons (in addition to being an important element in a positive industrial policy). This implies a monetary union and eventually a common currency. A powerful role for the Community institutions in the raising of loans from the market to finance community expenditure of a capital nature and to cover the Community's short-term financial requirements could make a major contribution to the evolution of an adequate capital market. Meade has pointed out that an integrated banking system can also be very helpful as an equilibrator in relation to the flow of short-term capital.[30]

(g) *Co-ordination of member countries' monetary, budgetary and incomes policies.* Since tendencies towards inflation or deflation in one member country will have a direct impact on the other members, and they have renounced the main weapons with which they could formerly defend themselves, co-ordination of national monetary and budgetary policies may be required, in order to ensure that member countries do not export their problems to each other. Tinbergen makes a useful division of national policy instruments into "supporting instruments," which act in the same direction on the well-being of all the countries concerned, for example public-spending in a time of economic depression in all member countries; and "conflicting instruments," whose use by country A conflicts with the objectives of other countries' policies, for example devaluation at a time of depression in all member countries. Supporting instruments are suitable for decentralized, or national, use and conflicting instruments for centralized, or co-ordinated, use.[31]

The first six of these areas of policy would seem to be the main elements in the equilibrating of inter-regional balance-of-payments deficits, or surpluses, in advanced national economies, without harmful effects on the growth of the regions that have structural deficits and indeed stimulating their growth. The seventh item belongs to an economic union, where the separate monetary, budgetary, and perhaps incomes, policies of the member countries remain important. Taken together, the seven items offer a framework in which one could be fairly certain that both short-term and long-term balance-of-payments problems of member countries would be met without unnecessary or prolonged restriction of the economic growth of a country or of important regions within it.

The fact must be faced that this would imply a high degree of positive integration. The common market in question, in our case the European Community, would have to develop its own major policies on a wide range of subjects: regional, transport, social, capital market (including the raising of public loans), monetary, fiscal (including the raising of money for community purposes), industrial and technological. It would also have to co-ordinate the monetary, budgetary and incomes policies of the member countries. These represent most of the elements of economic union.

The failure of the Community to achieve much in this direction so far has been attributed earlier to the relative ease in general, in post-war Europe, of securing agreement upon and implementing negative integration, and to the hostility of General de Gaulle, combined with passivity of most member governments, to the strong institutional system that is necessary if substantial positive integration is to be brought about. I also mentioned that doctrinal reservations of the German neo-liberals, and of Dr. Erhard in particular, about some of the aspects of positive integration. The latter is a special case of a general problem that constitutes one of the greatest obstacles to positive integration. This is the problem of agreement upon the objectives of policy and, in so far as the instruments are not only technical means but also have implications with respect to ends, also upon the use of instruments to secure the objectives.

The general problem is briefly considered by Tinbergen.[32] In relation to the Community in particular, Denton has analysed the main differences between the French "planning school" and the German neo-liberals that have been a part of the context for policy discussions and decisions, or failures to decide.[33] Recognizing the fundamental importance of this problem in the long run, the Community has set up the medium-term Policy Committee, which produced the first Medium-term Economic Policy Programme that was approved by the Council of Ministers in 1967,[34] and a second, Supplementary Programme in March 1968. This is a promising start, and it is encouraging that in the midst of all its current difficulties the Community has been capable of doing something about its basic long-term problems. But it is only a small beginning along what must certainly be a long and uphill road.

In the face of difficulties as great as these, the reader may ask himself why one should bother to try to overcome them. Some of the arguments for negative integration were considered earlier in this paper and need not be repeated here; it may be enough to say that it is hard to envisage a return to national autarky. My argument for positive integration has been largely confined to one objective: balance-of-payments equilibrium without unnecessary restriction of growth, and, although there are powerful arguments in relation to other objectives, it seems to me that this alone shows that negative integration is unsatisfactory, and may well prove to be objectionable, unless it is accompanied by a substantial measure of positive integration. This view, and the failure of the Community to undertake the necessary positive integration, was recently confirmed by Uri in an assessment of contemporary experience in the Community.

> The course of the Common Market is something of a disappointment. . . . Stagnation now prevails in all member countries except Italy. . . . The peril of a pure and simple liberalisation of trade—the propagation of deflation—was fully realised [by those who conceived the idea of the Community], hence the importance attached to common economic policy. . . . The freer trade is, the more serious the effect . . . [but] coordination is hardly more than a word. . . . The Brussels Commission, more often than not, is content to advise each country to do no more than it is prepared to accept—which will normally be what it intended to do anyway. To request member states to pay attention to the impact of their policies on their partner is generally wishful thinking.[35]

8 / CONCLUSION

The European Community has virtually completed its customs union and has gone far towards the removal of non-tariff discrimination too, and hence towards the establishment of the Common Market. It has formed a common agricultural policy, an unsatisfactory but nevertheless an effective one, and it has, with the conclusion of the Kennedy Round, carried out a major trade negotiation. It has institutions and a capable civil service that could be effective if member governments had the will to let them work, though this condition may imply that, in order to be effective, the central institutions need to be strengthened. It has blueprints, more or less far advanced, for policies that comprise many of the aspects of positive integration.

But the Community so far has, apart from the agricultural

policy and the Kennedy Round, no major achievements of positive integration, that is of policies that go beyond the removal of discrimination. Positive integration, particularly to solve the balance-of-payments problems of member countries now that their national economic defences have been removed, may be necessary to the success and even the survival of the Community. This may require (a) major common policies at Community level over a wide range of key subjects, including regional, social, monetary and fiscal policies with the corresponding fiscal and loan-raising powers, and (b) the co-ordination of the monetary, budgetary and incomes policies of the member states.

My contention is that the Community, having for good reasons made negative integration effective, will find itself compelled to swallow this large dose of positive integration or seriously to water down the Common Market that has been achieved. If this is so, two basic questions that remain are "Will the Community regain the political momentum, and find the economic means, to establish these essential elements of economic union?" and "What part, if any, will Britain play in this process?"

Notes:

[1] Paper prepared for the Bailey Conference, January 1968, at the London School of Economics.

[2] B. Balassa, *The Theory of Economic Integration*, Allen and Unwin, 1961, pp. 1–2.

[3] *Ibid.*, p. 2.

[4] J. Tinbergen, *International Economic Integration*, Elsevier, Amsterdam and Brussels, 1954, p. 122. Tinbergen defines negative integration as "the elimination of certain instruments of international economic policy" and a "positive policy of integration" as "supplementary measures in order to remove inconsistencies that may exist between the duties and taxes of different countries," plus "positive action in the field of production," in order to put through a "reorganization programme," i.e., to deal with the problems of transition. Thus Tinbergen bases his distinction between the two terms on whether policy instruments are to be eliminated or new policies formed, whereas I base mine on whether the purpose is to remove discrimination or to maximize welfare in other ways.

[5] Balassa, *op. cit.*, p. 7.

[6] J. Viner, *The Customs Union Issue*, New York, 1950.

[7] See, for example, J. E. Meade, *The Theory of Customs Unions*, Amsterdam, 1955.

[8] *Ibid.*, pp. 107–14.

[9] See, for example, T. Scitovsky, *Economic Theory and Western European Integration*, Stanford University Press, Stanford, 1958, pp. 72, 73: "In the literature of the subject much importance is attached to the question whether or not the cost reduction renders production within the union cheaper than it is in the outside world. In the long run, however, this seems irrelevant, from the point of view either of the union or of the world as a whole." See also B. Balassa, *The Theory of Economic Integration*, Allen and Unwin, 1961, p. 14: "In evaluating the effects of economic integration, we shall take dynamic efficiency as the primary success indicator." See also R. G. Lipsey, "The Theory of Customs Unions: a General Survey," *Economic Journal*, September 1960, pp. 511–13.

[10] An unpublished paper, quoted by Scitovsky, *op. cit.*, pp. 64–67.

[11] H. G. Johnson, "The Gains from Free Trade with Europe: An Estimate," *Manchester School*, September 1958.

[12] *Britain and Europe*, The Economist Intelligence Unit, 1957.

[13] *Ibid.*, p. 511.

[14] *The Free Trade Area Option*, Maxwell Stamp Associates, 1967.

[15] *The Times*, 1 May 1967.

[16] *Ibid.*, Part II.

[17] D. Swann and D. L. McLachlan, *Concentration or Competition: A*

European Dilemma? Chatham House/PEP European Series No. 1, 1967, pp. 7–13.

18 *Ibid.*, Part III.

19 In, for example, *The Economic Development of Latin America and Its Principal Problems*, Economic Commission for Latin America, United Nations, 1950; and "Commercial Policy in the Underdeveloped Countries," *American Economic Review, Papers and Proceedings*, May 1959.

20 P. Streeten, *Economic Integration: Aspects and Problems*, Sythoff, Leyden, 1961, pp. 53–67.

21 J. E. Meade, *op. cit.*, pp. 114, 115.

22 The system is described in T. K. Warley, *Agriculture: The Cost of Joining the Common Market*, Chatham House/PEP European Series No. 3, 1967. See also Paper No. 10, pp. 286–95.

23 See Paper No. 11, pp. 319–22.

24 See A. Forsyth, *Steel Pricing Policies*, PEP, 1964, pp. 348–59.

25 See Paper No. 4, pp. 119–29.

26 See Paper No. 6, pp. 178–86.

27 See Paper No. 12, pp. 340–48.

28 See D. Dosser and S. S. Han, *Taxes in the EEC and Britain: The Problem of Harmonization*, Chatham House/PEP European Series No. 6, 1968.

29 See Paper No. 11, pp. 313–19.

30 See J. E. Meade, *Problems of Economic Union*, Allen and Unwin, 1953, pp. 40–41. Part II of this book contains a useful discussion of the balance-of-payments problem in an economic union, as does Chapter 1 of Meade's *Theory of Customs Unions*, Part II of Scitovsky, *op. cit.*, and Chapter 12 of Balassa, *op. cit.*

31 Tinbergen, *op. cit.*, pp. 98, 99.

32 *Op. cit.*, pp. 101–3.

33 G. R. Denton, *Planning in the EEC: The Medium-term Economic Policy Programme of the European Economic Community*, Chatham House/PEP European Series No. 5, 1967, pp. 9–21. See also Paper No. 12, pp. 332–36.

34 See Denton, *op. cit.*, pp. 9–21.

35 P. Uri, "Stagnation Threatens the Common Market," *The Times*, 29 September 1967.

THEORETICAL APPROACHES TO EUROPEAN INTEGRATION

BY MARIE-ELISABETH DE BUSSY, HÉLÈNE DELORME,
AND FRANÇOISE DE LA SERRE

During the past two decades, political scientists in the United States have attempted to develop a theory of integration, frequently using European integration as their most fruitful case study. Their efforts to develop analytical tools and formal models, drawing upon such fields as cybernetics and economics, are summarized by three French scholars in the following chapter. As the writers show, the search for a theory of general validity has led to a clearer understanding of the crucial features of integration in Western Europe itself. This chapter was originally published as an article, "Approches théoriques de l'intégration européenne," in Revue Française de Science Politique, *Vol. XXI (3), June 1971, pp. 615–53. It is reprinted here by permission of the journal. The translation is by Helen Baz.*

The phenomenon of European integration has been studied in Europe mainly by historians, jurists and economists, whereas American researchers have seen it more in terms of political science.* As Karl Kaiser observes, political research in Europe is mainly concerned with institutions and is often confined to the setting of the nation-state, or considers the latter as the basic unit of international life, while in the United States the political scientists, because of a closer connection between the political and social sciences, are more interested in the transnational forces which work on the integration process.[1] They have concentrated their efforts on the study of changing attitudes, particularly of the élite groups, and on research into indicators capable of measuring the degree of integration attained.

This development in European integration studies has grown up around a new concept of the future direction of theoretical research. Theory is seen as neither a philosophy of history concerned with clarifying the evolution of relations among states, nor as political thought, which has proved to be partisan and normative, but is conceived in terms of a scientific approach which on an empirical basis, by the scientific study of observable phenomena, attempts to discover the principal variables, to explain the behavior, and to reveal the types of relations that are characteristic among national units.[2] Thus American researchers, on the basis of an empirical analysis, have tried to work out conceptual frameworks enabling them to raise questions, direct future research, and advance hypotheses which must be tested against reality.

The object of the present study is not to criticize existing theories nor to formulate new ones but to review and place them in relation to each other. The analysis is confined to a few authors, selected because they are the most representative of the different currents of thought and because their theoretical development is the most comprehensive and the most advanced.

* This article was prepared by the European Politics section of the Centre for Studies of International Relations, under the direction of Pierre Gerbet. Françoise de la Serre presents the views of K. Deutsch and the work of D. Puchala; Hélène Delorme the functional integration theory; and Marie-Elisabeth de Bussy reviews the work of L. Lindberg.

I
EUROPEAN INTEGRATION AND SOCIAL COMMUNICATIONS
K. DEUTSCH'S APPROACH

Studies of the phenomenon of European integration are to be found in the early work of Deutsch devoted to research into attempts at regional organization and have served, to a certain extent, as a test of his theoretical propositions concerning integration in general. This approach is characterized by the importance which Deutsch attaches to the conditions necessary for the birth and development of integration and is marked, on the methodological level, as is most of his work, by the use of cybernetic schemata.

A / Concepts and Methods

The small book of Deutsch's entitled *Political Community at the International Level*,[3] published in 1954, already reveals the interest of its author in the formation of political communities on an international level and is a theoretical essay forming the backcloth to most of the later research work carried out by him and by his team of workers. *Political Community and the North Atlantic Area*,[4] the product of a collective project undertaken at Princeton University, takes up and develops, several years later, all the hypotheses and propositions of 1954, to formulate a general study of the process of integration and especially of the conditions necessary for setting it in motion. The conclusions drawn from this are then applied to the example of the North Atlantic area.

The aim of the authors is to study the phenomenon of regional integration based on the examination of thirty-three case histories spread over two or three generations, with the intention of applying past experience to present needs. The analysis is based on several key definitions related essentially to the terms "integration" and "security community." Political integration is seen here as being the realization in a certain territory of a "sense of the community accompanied by institutions and practices—formal or otherwise—strong enough and widespread enough to assure for a 'long' time dependable expectations of 'peaceful change' among its population."[5] A group in a state of integration such as that which has just been defined constitutes a "security community." There are two types of these: first, pluralistic security communities, retaining in quasi-totality their sovereignty but determined to resolve any possible conflicts in a peaceful manner; and secondly, amalgamated security communities which are unitary states, unions of states, and federal states. According to this definition, Sweden and Norway represent, at the present time, the pluralistic type of security community, and the United States the amalgamated community.

The analysis of these different types of security community existing in the past has enabled the authors to determine the conditions necessary for their constitution. Nine conditions are seen to be necessary, within this context, for the emergence of amalgamated communities: compatibility of values in respect to political behavior, common life-style, hopes of closer economic links and greater gains, an increase in political and administrative capacity of at least some of the participants,[6] a high level of economic growth, the existence of social communication links among different regions and among different social strata, the enlargement of political élites, mobility of people, multiplicity of communication, and exchange flows. In addition, three other conditions are desirable: an equilibrium between communication and exchange flows, frequent change of roles among groups, and mutual predictability of behavior. This list of conditions indicates the priority given by the authors to the attitudes of social groups whose actions, according to them, are the determining factor in the setting in motion of the process of integration. Indeed, the latter is analyzed in terms of "communication networks which transmit messages, exchange information, carry out certain functions and accumulate experience."[7] Deutsch has always favored this approach, which is inspired by the science of social communications and is notable for its use of a certain number of quantifiable indicators: he first applied it, on the domestic level, to his study of nationalism,[8] and then later on developed its possibilities in his basic work, *The Nerves of Government*.[9] The value of these methods for the study of international integration movements has been demonstrated by Deutsch on various occasions, in particular, in two contributions to collective works. In one article, he analyzes the importance of this approach in the general study of the theory of international relations,[10] while in the other, he uses it to clarify the phenomenon of political integration.[11]

This rapid survey of the work carried out by Deutsch and his team of research workers tends to place his studies on the phenomenon of European integration within the wider framework of his theoretical and methodological preoccupations concerning the phenomenon of integration in general. It explains both the importance attached by the author to integration, seen essentially as an intensification of the social communications network, and the search for indicators capable of measuring it.

B / Diagnosis of European Integration

The observation and analysis of European integration by Deutsch and his colleagues are the central themes of two works published in 1967, and which there is no reason to separate in this present essay, since both of them are the products of the same inquiry.[12]

The research work of Deutsch and his team on the phenomenon of European integration falls within the over-all framework of a study on French and German attitudes toward armaments and disarmament.[13] The study set out to establish whether or not the national policies of France and West Germany toward these issues were liable to be modified as a result of progress made in the field of European integration. The answer to this basic question implied a rise in the level of integration. It is mainly the collective work, *France, Germany and the Western Alliance*, which supplies the elements of the reply, which *Arms Control* views in the light of the initial inquiries.

The aim of the authors is to establish a diagnois of European integration not by studying the manifestations of formal integration but by analyzing the indicators of real behavior. With this in mind, they collected a large amount of information on a variety of subjects, from which they then extracted by different methods a mass of quantifiable data concerning various areas: interviews with French and German executives, opinion surveys, analyses of the content of different newspapers, and, above all, statistics in respect to different international transactions measuring real behavior (commerce, travel, student exchanges, postal traffic).

The conclusions of the Yale team of researchers are based on the combined exploitation of these five sources of information, but we shall not go into detail here as to the methods used by the authors; they are, in any case, explained at length in their works. One point in particular is worth mentioning, however, because of its originality as well as the criticisms and developments which followed from it. It concerns the index of "relative acceptance," which illustrates the importance attached by Deutsch to the application of quantitative methods to the social sciences.[14] This statistical tool, whose method of calculation is explained at length in an article by Deutsch and Savage,[15] is applied here extensively to the measurement of dissymmetries in commercial transactions.

Deutsch's intention in using this method of calculation is to go beyond the evidence normally produced by examining commercial transactions only. The analysis he makes of transactions among present members of the Common Market for the period 1890–1963, after a comparison with the transactions of other groups of countries (Anglo-American zone, Scandinavia), leads him to two conclusions. Firstly, that Western Europe has been integrated since 1890 and possibly even earlier; secondly, that the rhythm of this integration has slowed down since 1957–58. Although the total volume of transactions since 1958 has undoubtedly increased in absolute figures, the level of growth, according to him, is not superior to the rate one might expect from the general growth of transactions and the increase in productivity. It cannot be attributed to a "structural" transformation. Identical conclusions are reached by the authors after examination of other data, such as the intensive content-analysis carried out, with the help of computers, of two hundred articles from different national newspapers, showing a declining interest in plans for European unification over the period 1953–63. Equally, the opinion surveys carried out in France and West Germany for the period 1952–62 indicate that public opinion in these countries attaches more importance to national problems than to European questions, and this despite the fact that Deutsch takes into account the progress made between 1957 and 1962 in establishing the image of a unified Europe among these same publics.[16] Finally, interviews with French and German élite groups (441 in France, 650 in the Federal German Republic) also reveal the nationalist opinions held by French executives and the open or latent differences existing between them and their German counterparts. As a result of the combined analysis and exploitation of these various elements, considered by Deutsch and his team as the indicators of integration, the authors reach a number of conclusions, some of which concern the recent evolution of European integration and its future prospects.[17] They are argued in almost identical terms in the different works mentioned above. For example, in *France, Germany and the Western Alliance*, they are explained as follows:

> The movement toward structural European unification since 1957 has been largely halted or very much slowed down. The next decade of European politics is likely to be dominated by the politics of nation-states, and not by any supranational European institutions. . . . In the question of European unification we are at the most in a position to expect the revival after 1975 of the movement of the 1950's. Until then, we may expect that the present level of evolution will be maintained and will progress slightly.[18]

Two significant points emerge from these conclusions: firstly, the statements in respect to Europe are equally applicable to

Deutsch's wider vision of the international system: the international system, in fact, seems to be characterized by the growing independence of national states, which are themselves becoming more and more integrated, and by the decline of integration both at a regional and world level.[19]

The other observation concerns the choice of indicators capable of measuring political integration and the relation which exists, according to the author, between the process of social assimilation and political integration. In other words, they are trying to show the links which exist between the empirical studies, which we have just discussed, and the theoretical formulations which preceded and followed the appearance of the two works dealing more specifically with European problems.

C / Presentation of a Model: Social Assimilation and Political Integration

It seems, therefore, that for Deutsch the European Community has become a "security community" in so far as the hypothesis of a conflict in this region must apparently be ruled out, but a "pluralistic" security community since the states retain their sovereignty in political and military affairs.[20] On the other hand, the passage toward a more elaborate form of integration leading to an amalgamated security community demands, according to the author, other conditions, already presented, as we have seen, in *Political Community and the North Atlantic Treaty*, and later regrouped as follows: mutual relevance, compatibility of values and hopes of common gains, solidarity and mutual responsiveness, common identity and common loyalty.[21] It is the realization or the non-realization of these conditions that the indicators referred to in the European case set out to test. It is worth noting that they refer, for the most part, to the attitudes of social groups. Thus, for example, mutual relevance is measured in terms of the volume of transactions and of the different communications, while the degree of common generalized loyalty is determined by content analyses, public opinion surveys, interviews, etc.

We are now in a better position to understand, *a posteriori*, on the one hand, the choice of indicators used to carry out a diagnosis of the state of European integration, and on the other, the pessimistic nature of this diagnosis, since Deutsch sees social assimilation, which he chooses to measure by these indicators, as a preliminary to political integration. This thesis, which is implicitly argued in the case of European integration, was developed in the model of political integration proposed by Deutsch in 1968.[22] It gives priority, as in his previous works, to the relation between social assimilation and political integration both in respect to the conditions necessary for integration and to the integration process itself. Moreover, no separation exists, according to Deutsch, between the conditions necessary for integration and the processes themselves since the latter may at any given moment be merged with one another and bring the movement toward integration to the take-off stage.

Compared to an assembly-line process, the integration process develops around a core area made up of one or more political units, and presupposes the existence of a regional transnational population which Deutsch defines as a population with the probability of experiencing interaction, acquiring common experiences, and possessing similar preferences, hopes, and achievements.[23] The constitution of such a population is accomplished through a learning process, in the course of which the participants—élite groups and masses—in response to mutually beneficial transactions, adopt styles of behavior and habits which they believe will lead them to obtain further advantages. They learn to understand each other, to trust each other, and to anticipate new advantages to be gained from their identical perception of common problems and solutions. This phase of cooperation brings the integration process to the stage of political development through the creation of supranational institutions which, in turn, bring about various changes in the political system, since the attention and action of the actors (parties, interest groups, élites) are transferred from the national level to the community level.

The basic originality of Deutsch's contribution lies, for the moment, in the connection which exists, according to him, between social assimilation and political integration, and in the methods he uses to measure this integration. This contribution to the study of European integration has quite clearly aroused a number of different reactions and criticisms and has encouraged further research.

D / Development and Criticisms

We shall not be discussing in this article the development and polemics arising out of the application of quantitative methods to the study of international relations, even though Deutsch and his team have made abundant use of this type of technique to measure a certain number of transactions and to analyze from this angle the phenomenon of European integration.[24] Nor shall we be discussing various works which, although inspired by the methods and techniques of Deutsch, have only an indirect bearing on the study of European integration and on the theoretical approach based on the analysis of transaction flows.[25]

We shall, however, be examining the research work of Donald J. Puchala and Hayward R. Alker, who are more explicitly concerned with the propositions raised by Deutsch relating to the formation of an international community. Although Puchala, in an early work,[26] believes, like Deutsch, that the transaction flows serve as indicators of social assimilation, considered as a preliminary stage in the development of a political community, later on, in a joint research project with Alker, he modifies his initial views.[27] The study of intra-European transaction flows for the period 1928–63, using, in particular, the relative acceptance index, worked out by Deutsch and further developed by Alker, which enables them to define the links which, according to them, exist between exchange flows and the formation of a community. They believe, in fact, that "the level of economic interaction between different countries constitutes a valid indicator of their political integration," but they insist on the necessity to corroborate the inferences based on the economic transactions by the use of a number of indicators[28] capable of measuring the multiple, permanent, and mutually beneficial relations which characterize the existence of a community. Above all, they emphasize that the validity of these indicators does not imply that there is a causal relationship between the transactions they bring to light and the existence of the community itself.[29] They are even ready to acknowledge that the existence of the Common Market is a reflection of political integration as well as being a factor contributing to its development. In this way, the values, as well as the limitations, of studying integration by the analysis of the transaction flows are highlighted as its application and development proceeds,[30] and this explains why the approach has been the object of various criticisms.

Some criticisms, such as those of Stanley Hoffmann, are not so much concerned with Deutsch's conclusions on European integration as with his approach to the phenomenon of integration. Others, particularly those raised by Inglehart, question both the diagnosis and the postulates of the author of *Arms Control.*

Despite the convergence of views of Deutsch and Hoffmann on the persistence and reinforcement of the nation-state,[31] Hoffmann's criticisms of Deutsch's approach should not be overlooked. He points out, in particular, the danger of confusion existing between the determination of common characteristics in different cases of regional integration and the definition of the conditions necessary for the emergence and development of this integration. He considers that not enough emphasis has been placed on the study of integration as a process, nor on the examination of a certain number of what he believes are determining variables: ideology, institutions, decision processes. There are certainly difficult to analyze in terms of communication networks, and the reservation on this methodological point completes the criticisms concerned, not with works directly related to the creation of Europe, but with the integration schemata proposed by the Princeton group in 1957.[32]

In contrast, Ronald Inglehart's criticisms deal specifically with the works published in 1967. They concentrate on three main points: divergencies in the exploitation of the data collected by Deutsch and his team, disagreement over the conclusions reached concerning the stagnation of the integration movement, and doubts about the validity of the proposed model.

The use of the relative acceptance index to measure transaction flows is one of the points questioned by Inglehart, based on the following reasoning: "Must we ignore the importance of the growth of transactions within the EEC because economic growth has taken place at the same time?"[33] Does more integration in Europe necessarily mean fewer transactions with the rest of the world? Taken to its logical conclusion, Deutsch's reasoning implies that increased integration leads to a kind of autarchy, since it seems to be based on a "zero sum" reasoning, the gain on the one hand being canceled out by an equivalent loss on the other.[34] Inglehart also questions Deutsch's conclusions concerning the reactions of public opinion and the attitudes of élites. He considers, still pursuing the same line of reasoning, that close attention to national problems does not necessarily preclude the formation of a European consensus and that the attachment shown by German élite groups toward the Atlantic Alliance does not in itself exclude any progression toward Europeanism. Inglehart, whose interest in the role of public opinion in the integration process[35] is well-known, has developed a thesis diametrically opposed to that of Deutsch, based on the exploitation of new data (particularly concerning the attitude of younger generations). According to him, "The European political climate as a whole favors the formation of a European movement at the present time, and this has increased rather than decreased since 1958."[36]

Despite these conclusions, which are similar to those of other observers,[37] the author recognizes that little progress has been achieved at the institutional level but places the ultimate responsibility for these setbacks on the personality and actions of General de Gaulle.[38] This analysis attributes to him alone the contradictory nature of prognostics concerning the future of the EEC.

Another criticism made by Inglehart, and other authors such as

William Fisher,[39] has more fundamental implications for integration theory. It concerns the causal relationship, suggested more or less implicitly by Deutsch, between the existing social system and the behavior of the political system. According to these authors, Deutsch does not specify the relation existing between the level of transactions or the orientation of attitudes and the growth of an integrated political system, so that he measures a certain number of independent variables influencing the process of integration without indicating the political effects which they are likely to have, especially at the stage of decision-making. In the absence of proof of a theoretical relation between social assimilation and political development, they question this direct causal link between two variables of the integration process. These critics also reproach Deutsch for not showing sufficient interest in certain variables which other authors, such as Ernst B. Haas, believe to be of fundamental importance.

II
THE THEORY OF FUNCTIONAL INTEGRATION

In his work *The Uniting of Europe: Political, Social and Economic Forces, 1950–1957*, published in 1958,[40] Haas adopts an original approach from two points of view.[41] First of all, he argues that it is less urgent to know to what extent an international system exists than to know how it is formed. Since the end of the Second World War, in fact, we have seen a regrouping of states into plurinational blocs. It is this evolution and not the result of it that should be considered as political integration, in other words, a "process whereby political actors in several distinct national settings are persuaded to shift their loyalties, expectations and political activities toward a new and larger center, whose institutions possess or demand jurisdiction over the preexisting national states."

Haas also claims that integration should no longer be studied on the global level, but within a regional framework, since experience shows that it is easier to form a community at this level. The analysis of concrete examples of regional integration should, according to him, precede the knowledge of the mechanisms of integration at the international level as a whole.[42]

After explaining the theory of functional integration, we shall examine the main criticisms of it, and then Haas's modifications to it.

A / Functional Integration, an Automatic Process

The theory of functional integration, developed from the time of the European Coal and Steel Community, can be defined as follows: Economic integration of countries such as those in Western Europe, if directed by central institutions, automatically culminates in a political community.

1/Economic Integration

Haas uses this expression to attract attention to the area in which the process of integration is set in motion: the economic area. Haas maintains that "the superiority of limited economic decisions over crucial political choices [is] permanent."[43] In fact, this "incremental"[44] approach corresponds to the pluralist, bureaucratic, and industrial structure of European countries. It is also easier to achieve since it does not necessitate similar political options, but merely a convergence of interests on the part of each of the participating nations.

According to Haas, the history of Europe since 1945 confirms this rule. "It was not the fear of the Soviet Union nor the envy of the United States which did the job. Slogans of the past glories of Charlemagne, of the popes, of western civilization were certainly heard, but they did not launch the ECSC . . . or the EEC. Converging economic goals embedded in the bureaucratic, pluralistic and industrial life of modern Europe provided the crucial impetus."[45]

2/The Structural Conditions

In order to be a valid conceptual framework, the theory of functional integration calls for a certain number of structural conditions such as those observed by Haas in Western Europe.

Societies in which it is applicable must, in the first instance, have a pluralistic social structure. Power should not be vested in a single group but should be shared alternatively by different groups in competition with each other.[46] This situation of "symmetrical heterogeneity"[47] favors the enlargement of the political framework since it enables the different groups to come in contact with allies in other nations.

The integration of a number of states also demands a consensus on basic values which must not be endangered by the political struggle. Haas explained the connection between politics and economics in 1967, when he noted: "The key politicians—Schuman, Adenauer, Spaak, Beyer, De Gasperi, Van Zeeland, Fanfani—had simply decided to leave the game of high politics and devote themselves to the building of Europe, to achieve more modest aims. And then the economic technician could play his role within the shelter of the politicians' support."[48]

Finally, functional integration develops successfully in societies which show a growing bureaucratization of decision mechanisms.[49] This type of decision, noticeable in the Common Market countries, facilitates the confrontation and unification of different views at a regional level because it provides a suitable framework for the intervention of European officials.

3/The Strategic Role of Central Institutions

According to Haas, the central institutions are the mainspring of the process of political integration: "While the coexistence of conflict and harmony within the same social system can, no doubt, be achieved without the attributes of a new national consciousness, the deliberate creation and perpetuation of a new national consciousness can hardly be expected to come about without the presence of formal governmental institutions and practices."[50]

His study of the ECSC allows him to define the type of central institutions which are desirable. The juridical form is not so important, according to Haas, as the capacity and will to exercise the functions carried out previously by member governments. He insists on three essential features: the independence of the new institutions, the possibility of extending their powers, and the links between the integrated sector and the rest of the economy.

Haas's intention, in the second place, is to show the double function fulfilled by the supranational administration. It contributes, on the one hand, to the breaking up of "the inherent autonomy of functional contexts,"[51] in other words, to preventing integration from being confined to the sector in which it first began. On the other hand, the leading élite groups have "a decisive manipulative role,"[52] since they encourage the transfer of the loyalties, interests, and activities of specific groups, with whom they have established direct contacts, toward the new decision center.

4/The Spill-over of Functional Integration

This makes possible the progression from economic union to political union. If such central institutions exist, Haas believes that "the progression from a politically inspired common market to an economic union and finally to a political union among states is automatic. The inherent logic of the functional process within a setting such as Western Europe can push no other way."[53]

Economic integration, in fact, sets in motion a process of gradual politicization: the decisions made by the central institutions lead the different groups to reorganize themselves at this level. The spill-over inherent in the process leads to a continuous extension of integration in all directions: toward groups which did not participate to begin with; toward the rest of the economic and political activity based on decisions which are no longer mere bargaining but are the product of a global concept;[54] toward foreign countries (Haas interprets the rapprochement between Great Britain and the Six in this light).[55] When the process is completed, a new political community has come into existence, which takes over all the functions exercised formerly by the states.

Conflicts encourage this spill-over.[56] Disagreements over a common decision incite the political actors to intensify their pressure on the new center of decision in order to influence its actions. The new community is, consequently, strengthened following the crisis which has enabled it to redefine its common aims.

The spill-over, discovered by Haas, applies to all decisions. Haas believes, in fact, that in industrial and technocratic societies, such as the Europe of the Six, it is no longer possible to make a distinction between economics and politics, and that they should be considered as belonging to the same continuum. This continuity makes possible the automatic progression from economic integration to political integration.

The integration process is completed when a new political community is constituted. Haas gives a precise definition to this stage of the process: a political community is a "condition in which specific groups and individuals show more loyalty to their central political institutions than to any other political authority, in a specific period of time and in a definable geographic space."[57] So the end product is certainly a new state, probably a federation, similar to those which already exist in Europe and the United States.

5/Political and Theoretical Scope of This Approach

The theory of functional integration reveals the strategic role played by institutions in the process of integration. As Michael Banks observes: "Where functionalist doctrine assumed that political community formation would be a natural consequence of technical cooperation, Monnet and the neo-functionalists realized that the political side needed a push, and gave it one . . . in setting up cross-national pressure groups to speed the process."[58] Haas's position, therefore, lies midway between the functionalist and federalist approaches.

On the other hand, the conceptual framework of Haas seems better suited than strict functionalism to the study of the intermediate period during which a plurinational community is constituted. In particular, Haas's dynamic definition of integration as a process has been widely accepted.

These two elements explain why Haas's theoretical ideas have gained such a sympathetic hearing both from the theorists and from the men—politicians and technicians—dedicated to the success of the Europe of the Six. It is no coincidence that his theories originally closely resembled, if they did not directly derive from, the actions taken by men like Jean Monnet, Walter Hallstein or Sicco Mansholt.

Research into regional integration has developed by adopting the methods perfected by Haas and by continuing studies in the sectors he had indicated. For example, the early research work of Leon N. Lindberg, as presented in his publication of 1963,[59] was situated within this framework. While it bears a close resemblance to Haas's approach, especially in respect to the conditions of integration,[60] it concentrates on the study of decision-making and reveals the original nature of the community system.

Lindberg agrees with Haas that integration is a process, but attaches little importance to the determination of the final stage of this process, and makes no explicit reference to an ideal federal-type system.[61] He prefers to analyze European communities in terms of an institutional system *sui generis* and to consider political integration as "the development of devices and processes for arriving at collective decisions by means other than autonomous action by national governments."[62]

However—and it is precisely on this point that he parts company with Haas—it seems to him "that it is logically and empirically possible that collective decision-making procedures involving a significant amount of political integration can be achieved without moving towards 'a political community' as defined by Haas."[63]

This attitude leads him to put forward his own definition of political integration, slightly modifying that of Haas. He sees it as a double process. On the one hand, "nations forego the desire and ability to conduct foreign and key domestic policies independently of each other, seeking instead to make *joint decisions* or to *delegate* the decision-making process to new central organs"; on the other hand, "political actors in several distinct settings are persuaded to shift their expectations and political activities to a new center."[64] This definition shows the importance attached by Lindberg to decision-making. According to him, the two methods of decision-making are closely linked, since the existence of a delegated decision-making process conditions the progress of shared decision-making. It also emphasizes the response of political actors to this new method of decision, their new way of perceiving their interests and their behavior in each of the states concerned. The repercussions at community and national levels of these two decision processes are examined by means of several case studies, especially by the examination of the development of the common agricultural policy.[65]

Furthermore, Lindberg's preoccupations concerning the transformation and persistence of the community system places him, from this period onward, in the line of research originated by David Easton,[66] and gives some indication of the direction his later work is likely to take.[67]

B / Criticisms
The crises experienced by the Europe of the Six, like the new developments in regional integration, have revealed certain defects in the functional approach.

1 / Criticisms by Economists
A study of results obtained by the Six have led economists like Bela Balassa and Lawrence Krause[68] to conclude that the advantages derived from a large market can be obtained without necessarily having to create new institutions. According to these authors, all that is needed is to free domestic trade and to set up a foreign customs tariff. "A 'hidden hand,' toward policy coordination, is directed by the market mechanism and it has proven to be very effective with the EEC."[69]

Balassa also remarks that "an intergovernmental approach seems sufficient for the efficient working of an economic union without a unification of the institutional structure."[70] This possibility is discussed in the work of André Marchal.[71] This author believes that, since a political Europe can emerge only from the development of the economic solidarity of the Six by the application of common policies, the main obstacle to overcome is not nationalism but free trade.

Haas, apparently, foresaw the possible effect of such a liberal customs union when he wrote that "planning, and especially democratic planning, would be the simplest way to insure an ever increasing scope to the new agencies. If the groups . . . were consistent champions of free trade and free enterprise, no institutional future whatever would accrue to a High Authority looking to these groups for support."[72] But he confines himself to observing that no group would defend such a liberal position.

2/Stanley Hoffmann's Criticisms

The second critical analysis of the neo-functional approach was made by Stanley Hoffmann. It is interesting from two points of view: it is extremely articulate; and it preceded Haas's revision of his model,[73] and no doubt contributed to it.

Hoffmann bases his analysis on a different theoretical concept of international relations: he challenges the theory of assimilation of economic and political questions argued by Haas. According to him, on the contrary, a clear distinction should be made in foreign policy between problems which are economic, sectoral and quantifiable and purely political problems, which he defines as those concerned with the vital interests of diplomacy and national strategy, and which involve the nation as a whole.[74]

Hoffmann claims that this distinction makes it possible to define the area in which the logic of functional integration is applicable by limiting it. Although, according to him, states are ready to go along with functional integration in the economic field, this does not equally apply to political matters, where it is not possible to take such a risk, for a nation can win or lose everything at one go. "Consequently," Hoffmann concludes, "any theory which exaggerates the 'automatism' of the spill-over in integration must be rejected."[75]

Hoffmann also points out that Haas's analysis does not take

into account the outside world. He considers that this omission prevents this theory from explaining the setback in political integration, caused by two characteristic elements in the present international system. The first is the global nature of the system. According to Hoffmann, the present international system is built entirely around East–West relations of major tension.[76] European integration is, thus, subordinated to the conflicting opinions dividing the Six in their common attitude toward the outside world. The regional sub-system becomes a lever in the rivalry of its members in international affairs.

The international system is also characterized by the nuclear balance of power and, consequently, by the stability of a bipolar world. Hoffmann believes that the nuclear threat reinforces the legitimacy of existing nation-states and is one of the factors contributing to the rebirth of a national consciousness in Europe. Haas had constructed his theoretical model after the success of the European policy conceived by men such as Jean Monnet. Hoffmann's criticism of him several years later based its arguments very largely on the actions of General de Gaulle in Europe. Both these considerations have led Haas to modify his original integration theory.

C / Functional Integration, a Dialectical Process

The necessity to take into account "the lessons learned from General de Gaulle,"[77] in other words, the evolution of the Common Market since 1958, as well as experiments in integration in other regions, has led Haas to modify his theory. This modification is apparent both in the basic concepts which have moved away from the federalist model implicit in his earlier approach and in the new concept of the logic of functional integration.

1 / Basic Definitions

The existing types of national communities no longer serve as indicators of political union, which henceforth is defined as "any arrangement under which existing nation-states cease to act as autonomous decision-making units with respect to an important range of politics."[78] This definition covers unitary states as well as federations and the Common Market, in which powers are "shared but not clearly divided."[79] No reference at all is made to juridical norms in the definition.

The new concept of integration seeks to be compatible with the fragmentation of loyalties of the individuals belonging to nations engaged in such a process. Haas uses this term, then, to qualify both the transitional period between the establishment of the economic community and its possible culmination into a political entity and the events which take place during this period (gradual politicization, transfer of aspirations, adaptation of the actors) and which engender political union. Integration is still a process but no longer involves a transfer of allegiance to a new entity.

2 / The Logic of Functional Integration

a) The logic of functional integration is a logic of probability and is no longer automatic. Economic integration is "a frail process, susceptible to reversal. And so integration can once more develop into disintegration."[80] Functional integration, in fact, is based on decisions which display three specific characteristics: they are gradual, in other words, confined to particular issues; they are non-oriented, that is, their political implications are not revealed; and they are functional in that they are based on a combination of pragmatic and temporary interests and not on a long-term agreement. In addition, the evolution of the functional integration process depends on a large number of variables, which Haas classified according to when they occur (before, during or after the negotiations for the creation of the union) without specifying their relations.[81]

So Haas has toned down considerably the socio-economic determinism of his early views. The automatism of functional logic has become a probability. "Automaticity, then, means that, all things being roughly equal, a 'high' scorer in our categories is likely to be transformed into some species of political union, even if some of its members are far from enthusiastic about this prospect when it is argued in purely political terms."[82]

b) Haas is not content with this ambiguous answer to the question of whether economic integration leads to political union. He tries to explain the twists and turns of the process of functional integration. In this respect, he considers that a vital role is played by one of the variables, namely, the actors' goals.

According to him, only one case conforms to the initial automatic model: when all the leaders (public and private) have economic aims and seek to maximize their material advantages by means of negotiations confined to technical matters. "Political parties and interest groups avoiding sharp ideological conflict are essential."[83] Once this agreement on basic issues is broken, the observer feels the same uncertainty about it as he does toward the other cases.

Haas's approach can be criticized in terms of a different theoretical concept of international relations. This is the view argued by Hoffmann, who does not accept the socio-economic determinism of the neo-functional theory but, in the tradition of writers like Raymond Aron, makes a distinction between political order (high politics or power politics) and economic order (low politics or welfare politics), and gives priority to the former.

This distinction does not seem convincing to some observers who note that its frontiers vary according to the type of country being analyzed. Nye, for instance, in his studies on regional integration in Central America and Africa, shows how, in these areas, problems of economic organization run up against the same difficulties and call for the same type of solutions as do strategic problems in Europe.[84] The distinction between these two orders would seem to apply more to the attitudes involved than to the areas they cover.

These authors have thus developed a critique which questions neither the functionalist theory of integration nor the limits within which it is valid, but which seeks to improve it by correcting the three main imperfections which it presents, in their view. This approach does not take into account external factors, any more than the first version did. It does not allow for an evaluation of how the global international system affects the sub-system in the process of integration. Some authors have tried to suggest frameworks which take into consideration the external variables. The work published by Etzioni is certainly more successful in incorporating the external variables within a functional framework. Etzioni integrates the external variable by examining the competing forces in integration (external and internal) and the degree of internalization of these forces.[85]

In the second place, Haas's theory does not specify the relations between the privileged factor in the concrete analysis—the goals of public and private actors—and the other variables in the general typology. This omission is due to the fact that the links between variables are not specified. The work of Nye on regional integration attempts to fill this gap. It makes a distinction between a dependent variable (economic integration) and other independent variables which explain the variations of the former. But up to now, Nye has been more concerned with the growth of integration among developing countries than in European integration.[86]

The third observation on Haas's theory relates to the composite nature of the concepts used. Nye has already raised this problem in respect to the initial model. "The concept . . . of interdependence can be broken down into economic integration (formation of a transnational economy), social integration (formation of a transnational society), and political integration (formation of a transnational political interdependence). These three can in turn be broken down into more interesting and more useful sub-types, each associated with a clear measurement."[87] The same observation could apply to the variable of "actors' goals," to which Haas attaches particular importance. This could also be broken down into a number of sub-categories. Such a clarification would show that this variable is as much, if not more, a consequence rather than a variable: the actors' goals are in particular—as Haas noted in his initial study—widely influenced by the development of the integration process itself. If considered as a privileged variable of this process, they would perhaps enable us to estimate the effects of the Gaullist policy on the Europe of the Six in the 1960s, but it confines the theory of functional integration within a circular explanation.

III
NEW DIRECTIONS IN RESEARCH ON EUROPEAN INTEGRATION

At the present time a number of studies, in varying degrees of development, seem to be moving research on European integration in new directions less closely associated with the attitudes based on the analysis of transactions or decision-making which we have just discussed. They appear to have certain reservations about causal theories of integration and to exclude any form of social or functional determinism in the development of the process.

European integration is viewed as a complex phenomenon, with multiple dimensions; its evolution, in contrast to the forecasts of the fifties, necessitates the working out of new schemata and an improvement in methods of investigation.[88] As examples of these new directions in research, we shall examine the development in the work of two researchers belonging to the "schools" already discussed.

A / Donald Puchala's Draft of an Integration Model

Puchala proposes, not a new theory, but a model based on various approaches which, according to him, are not incompatible but complementary. The model seeks to establish the interaction between the processes of social assimilation and political development, and to determine and measure the evolution of the variables considered to be significant in the development of the process.

1/Statics and Dynamics of Integration

Despite theoretical differences which still exist between specialists as to the "why" and "how" of European integration, Puchala reckons that a very large measure of agreement exists on the facts which must be linked to this phenomenon, even if the relative importance attached to them varies according to the scholars concerned.[89]

The same agreement, in his view, applies to the structural, social and political characteristics of integration, which leads him to describe this phenomenon by a study of the institutions (functions and powers), the political régime (actors and stakes in the contest) and the transnational society (psychosociological foundations). Nor does he believe that the existence of systematic links[90] between these different characteristics, which develop in the course of the integration process, is in dispute.

Based on these elements, the author proposes an analysis in dynamic terms which, according to him, would be likely to gain the support of the majority of specialists and which presents regional integration as a process of transformation of the system at the level of international politics, involving various changes in the structure, style and climate of relations among states participating in the regional system. Puchala lists six changes: research into regional rather than national stability and security, the pursuit of cooperation rather than competition, amplification of communications, the replacement of suspicion by trust, similarity of interpretations and reactions in respect to regional and international problems, and the progressive elimination of the possibility of using force to resolve potential conflicts.[91]

Having described the integrated community and the transformations involved in the process, the author suggests that the movement toward integration is caused by the interaction of various political, social and psychological processes grouped together, by an extreme simplification, into a process of social assimilation on the regional level and a process of political development on the international level.[92]

By social assimilation, the author means a collection of mechanisms leading to a transnational society, in other words, to a regional population united by links of mutual understanding and trust. It takes place, in the first instance, among the élite groups and then spreads to the masses by means of the learning process, which is seen as the product of mutually beneficial interactions.

These learning processes, however, cannot in themselves account for the regional political development—in other words, the movement toward regional government and the birth of a supranational political régime with a coalition of political parties and interest groups. Puchala, by way of explanation, suggests several hypotheses based on "the complex interrelationships of several political, social and psychological processes" and puts forward the following schema:[93]

The origin of the process of political development—viewed as a continuous movement rather than a series of stages—is determined by the choice, made by the national élites, in favor of cooperative rather than competitive relations, insofar as, for domestic or foreign reasons, this cooperation seems advantageous to them. It emerges first of all in the classical intergovernmental organizations "where unanimous voting requirements and limited powers of international enforcement protect national sovereignty." The mutual advantages to be gained from cooperation strengthen, in turn, the assimilation which then exerts pressure in support of a development of the cooperation deemed necessary and desirable. "Herein lies a first causal link between international social assimilation and international political development. International political development beyond the initial 'cooperation with minimum risk' stage must be explained both in terms of a continuing need to cooperate and in terms of the international understanding and confidence developed during early phases of international cooperation."[94]

Just as the development of political institutions may be explained in terms of reciprocal relations between the two groups of the above-mentioned process, the appearance of a supranational political process can, similarly, be explained by the relation between the institutional growth and the organization of interests and of the competition of political and professional groups. At this stage of the explanation of the extension of supranational power, already attempted by various theoreticians,[95] Puchala returns to the analyses of Haas and Lindberg and is prepared to acknowledge with them that "while the existence of a regional institutional framework stimulates a regional political game, the game itself strengthens the framework."

Thus the proposed schema integrates previous approaches to the problem used by various specialists. By picking out certain categories of analysis and by isolating a number of variables, Puchala is trying to take into account the complexity of the phenomenon, not merely in terms of formal description, but also in terms of relationships. The principal originality of his work lies, therefore, in his refusal to accept any causal explanation of integration, based on variables considered in isolation, and in his research on methods likely to measure all the variables and their correlations.

2/The Analysis and Measurements of Variables

The proposed correlations between social assimilation and political development, put forward as a hypothesis to establish the nature of integration, lead the author to look for methods capable of analyzing and measuring these two variables, since there are clearly different stages in the formation of a community and different degrees in the evolution toward a supranational government. His work in this area runs parallel with that of Deutsch but goes beyond it insofar as the transactions studied by Deutsch reveal, according to him, only social assimilation and not integration as a whole. He, therefore, proposes, on the basis of a wider definition of the term "dealings," to extend this type of analysis to the process of political development and to create indicators which take into account the variety, quality and direction of the relations being studied.[96]

The indicators chosen by Puchala for the study of social assimilation differ only very slightly from those used by Deutsch and his team of workers, but it is worth noting the special importance attached by the author to the evolution of opinions and attitudes.[97] Furthermore, Puchala places particular emphasis on the variety of methods of measurement according to whether the research deals with the direction, intensity or other characteristics of the transactions being studied. He offers us, for this purpose, a table of available techniques.[98]

The examination of the process of political development, on the other hand, involves no longer simply a choice between various facts believed to be significant and to which access is relatively easy, but the creation of indicators capable of ascertaining the supranational structure and political evolution: the creation and development of central institutions, the volume of political transactions dealt with within this framework in relation to transactions outside it, the quantitative and qualitative increase in transactions between political and professional groups and among these groups and regional institutions, etc. The study undertaken by Puchala, using this approach, on Franco–German relations serves as an example of the development of some of these indices based on historical documentation.[99]

In conclusion, the importance attached by Puchala to the analysis of transaction flows calls for some comments on the role this method should play, according to him, in the study of the phenomenon of integration. On the one hand, the analysis of transactions, in the way Deutsch understood it in respect to European integration, seems inadequate to Puchala, since it illustrates only one of the components of integration and, consequently, he extends this type of analysis, by the appropriate means, to the political arena. In so doing, he is trying to achieve on the methodological level the synthesis he has established on the conceptual level. On the other hand, the author stresses the usefulness of this analysis from a descriptive point of view and reaffirms, in line with his model, that since no necessary causal link exists between certain types of transactions and integration it is dangerous to use this form of research for predictive ends. Nevertheless, he considers that the combined exploitation of various indicators could reveal the stages of the process (what comes before what). In a recent study, he makes use of this hypothesis in respect to Franco–German relations.

He suggests that in this particular case, as perhaps for the whole of the Common Market, the sequential development of integration has been as follows: increased transactions, institutional and political development, growth of support.[100]

B / The Application of the Theoretical Schema of David Easton to the European Community

Lindberg, who noted in 1966 that neither the assertions of the "logicians of diversity," who were looking forward to the triumph of the reborn and renovated national state, nor the expectations of the "logicians of integration," who anticipated the progressive advance of the Six toward a federal or quasi-federal system, have been justified by the facts, since the "nation state has not begun to wither away and yet it is no longer the sole framework of decision,"[101] believes it to be absolutely vital to take this situation into account in his research studies. He, therefore, tries to confront and to relate these different approaches by means of a macro-analysis, whose definitions and categories are borrowed from Easton.[102]

Lindberg, in fact, adopts Easton's definition of the political system conceived as "that system of interaction in any society through which binding or authoritative allocations are made or implemented,"[103] and considers, like him, that the problem of the persistence of political systems through change is of fundamental importance. Within the setting of the European Community, which is the system he has chosen to study, these allocations are constituted by decisions and the problem is seen in the following terms: "Is the European Community a system of interactions that constitutes a political system and can it persist over time, that is, does it have the capacities of responding to stress and perhaps expanding its scope?"[104] Since 1966, Lindberg has concentrated his research work on this double aspect of the problem.

The definition of the dimensions which bring into operation the concept of political integration allows him to identify the variables and the mechanisms whose interaction causes the system to evolve, and to suggest different models of the possible results of this evolution.[105]

1/The Dimensions of Political Integration

Lindberg sees the European Community as a new system of decision-making endowed with multiple characteristics varying one with another and over time, and undergoing a fairly high degree of political integration. In order to ascertain the nature of a multidimensional phenomenon, his description of it is as "multivariate" as possible, and he tries to clarify the dynamic interrelations which exist between the different characteristics of the system and which render each of them significant. His research work and proposals for indices to measure integration are directed toward these issues.[106] He attaches particular importance to two indicators: the scope of the division of political work (functional scope), which characterizes the system, and the institutional capacities which it reveals.

Functional scope includes both the areas in which European decisions exist, the different levels possible in the decision processes as well as their place of origin. His analysis for the years 1950–70 reveals that the nation-state is still the ultimate, dominant center of decision-making, although its monopoly has been under attack and there has been some progression in common action.

The institutional capacities of the system are apparent in the part played by the new structures of supranational decision-making and in the emergence of a series of regulations and norms which are respected by the political protagonists in their mutual behavior. This notion is comparable to that of the "régime" which, according to Easton's categories, constitutes, together with the "political community" and the "authorities," one of the three components of the system.[107] Community decisions are the result of a process, the basic element of which is the dialogue being carried on between the Commission and the Council of Ministers, and which is enmeshed in a complex network of formal and informal relations among the actors at the national or community level.

Lindberg rejects here the interpretation according to which the nature of the relations between Commission and Council or between Community and nation-states is basically one of conflict, the increasing powers of the one going hand in hand with the decreasing powers of the other; he maintains, on the contrary, that the Community came to birth and developed at least partially because the nation-states can no longer resolve certain problems on their own, and he considers that national governments continue to be one of the main sources of support and legitimacy for community institutions.

This development of new structures of decision and networks of interaction is based on an essential factor: the acceptance on a permanent basis by the political actors of certain "rules of the game" (procedural code) which determine, in particular, the way to resolve conflicts and which indicate who is responsible for negotiating an acceptable compromise. While the practice of "marathons" and package deals clearly involves a degree of rigidity, it serves as a means of redefining individual national interests "in terms of some notion of a collective goal or benefit"[108] with the prospect of a long-term equilibrium of gains and losses. The success of this method as a promoter of consensus among the participating countries clearly presupposes that the countries will maintain their commitment to, and interest in, the European Community and that their political leaders, élite groups and public opinion are inspired by feelings of mutual trust.

It is clear from all this that the ability of the system to make regular and effective decisions has had its up and downs.[109] The supranational institutions have revealed both their potential and the fragility inherent in their dependence upon the initiatives of their own personnel as well as on the governments which support these institutions.[110]

In choosing to assess the progress of European integration by means of these two main indicators—functional scope and institutional capacities—Lindberg reaches the conclusion, in contrast to Deutsch, that the greatest progress has been achieved since 1957–58. It is not surprising that these two authors should hold conflicting views, since their premises, the period studied, and the definitions used are different, and since their analyses are concerned with different aspects of the global reality constituted by the Community.

2/The Evolution of the System: Variables and Mechanisms

The fluctuations of functional scope and institutional capacities do not explain the reasons for the successes and failures experienced by the Community but serve as indicators which make it possible to assess the situation at any given moment. Believing that, by definition, the variations affecting them are a measure of the growth or decline of the system, in other words, the growth or decline of political integration, Lindberg isolates a certain number of variables and mechanisms whose dynamic interactions determine the internal evolution of the system.

It is important here to stress the difference in viewpoints existing between the analytical approach of Lindberg and that of Haas and Schmitter. The latter are concerned with the study of the general circumstances in which efforts being made toward an economic union can lead to political integration, thus revealing inter-systemic variations.[111] Their analysis clarifies the reasons which have enabled political integration to "take off" but does not explain why in the post-"take-off" stage, and within the political system itself, the successes have been very uneven, depending on the historical period as well as on the areas of activities studied. Lindberg, on the other hand, is primarily concerned with the internal variations of the system. Adopting Easton's categories of a systemic analysis, he presents the evolution of the Community (systems change) in the form of a model which isolates the most important variables: functional scope, institutional capacities, level of support, flow of demands, leadership.

The static role of support. It is worth knowing in what socio-political context the process of integration develops. For instance, do the existence of the links forged between the peoples of the Community and the degree of mutual identification and trust they achieve help to solve the common problem, although this identitive support bears no relation, according to Lindberg, to the growth of the system, in contrast to the concept argued by Deutsch, according to which the "growth of mutual identification is the characteristic of integration"?[112]

The support given to the system itself by its members (systemic support)[113] serves, on the other hand, as a true indicator of its capacity for growth. The existence of a consensus among public opinion and the élite groups concerning the legitimacy of the Community and the authority of its institutions (permissive consensus) is one of the conditions of the long-term persistence of the system and determines the "parameters of the decision process," in other words, the limits within which the actors can move fairly freely without running the risk of encountering strong opposition. The role of this support remains totally static, however, for the socio-political context, depending on whether it is hostile or congenial, constrains or facilitates the growth of the Community system, but does not determine it.[114] The action of the political actors in terms of demands and leadership has, in contrast, direct and tangible effects on the growth of the system.

The central role of demands and leadership. For a system as partial and incomplete as the European Community, the existence of a continuous flow of demands is a vital necessity even if such demands can be the source of tensions, especially when the system cannot respond successfully to them.

The impact of these demands varies enormously depending on the people from whom they originate and the nature of the goals and interests they are pursuing. In an analysis which has been strongly influenced by Haas, Lindberg draws a distinction between different types of actors according to whether their aims are "dramatic-political" or "incremental-economic,"[115] and according to the level of their sphere of influence and their different perceptions of the links existing between the interests they are seeking to defend and the integration movement. A modification of one or more of the constituent elements of this variable is all that is needed, therefore, to effect a change in the flow of demands.[116]

The political actors have an equally decisive influence on the growth of the system by providing it with the powers, imagination and energy necessary for the exercise of leadership, whether it originates in the Commission or in national governments. Lindberg emphasizes the fact that the Commission plays an essentially strategic role, while national governments act as both the "mediators of popular support" given to the system, and as its principal "gate-keepers," in that they control the demands formulated on the national level and, where necessary, reshape them before transmitting them to the community institutions.[117]

The mechanisms of coalition-building. If demands and leadership produce results, this is because these two variables serve as "activators" for the "mechanism of coalition-building,"[118] allowing the community system to "make decisions which induce growth." Here again, Haas's influence is very marked. Each of these mechanisms describes a different way in which various groups of actors come to realize that community decisions can bring them certain benefits. The best known of the four mechanisms described by Lindberg is functional spill-over, in which the actors are mobilized because of the functional link they perceive between various political tasks or areas, and this linkage mechanism applies particularly to the internal dynamics of economic integration. Nevertheless, there is nothing inevitable or automatic in the response of the actors, since the "autonomy of functional contexts" must be taken into consideration.

In other cases, it is a question of gaining the assent of a large number of political actors to a proposal or to a series of proposals by reconciling the conflicting interests through greater bargaining in a decision area or in a number of areas at the same time. The autonomy of functional contexts is, in turn, set in motion by the mechanism of the "actor socialization" in respect of the "immediate participants" of the decision process who, because of their mutual interactions, are led to intensify their commitments and their aspirations.[119]

The mechanism of feedback describes the impact of the outputs of the system on "the perceptions and behaviors of nonparticipants,"[120] who, following certain decisions, become more aware of the significance of the Community for them, or are even mobilized into action. This mechanism is thus closely linked to the various forms of support engendered by the prolonged existence and action of the system.

The important thing to remember is that none of these mechanisms can work without the will and ability of the political actors to make use of them, and that none of them has an automatic effect on the growth of the system.

3/Models of Change Resulting from the Evolution of the System

We are mainly concerned here with models of growth and equilibrium rather than with those of decline, since Lindberg's analysis tries to put forward a certain number of hypotheses about the conditions which favored them in the past and which make them probable in the future. He goes on to explain, however, that this approach does not justify any assumption about structure because it is concerned essentially with process and thus will have only a tangential relationship with the problem of projecting the future structure of the European system.[121]

The first growth model, which he calls the forward linkage model, implies that the members of the system have successfully complied with the obligations undertaken by them to participate in a shared decision process and have greatly increased the scope or institutional capacities of the system.[122] It is concerned with a purely quantitative change and an incremental growth which do not take into account any new variables.

The probability of forward linkage relies on a fundamental condition: the formation of a coalition of supporters, both among groups at the national level and among governments at the community level. The flow of demands will be stimulated if the prospect of growth contains the promise, in a particular sector, of a redistribution of the benefits in a form other than that of a "zero sum" operation. It is highly desirable that the actors mobilized should anticipate the gains to be derived from different aspects of the proposed policy—in other words, that their interests should not be identical but converging. The organization of this redistribution, according to the model, is the responsibility of the supranational leadership in the way it should be exercised by the Commission.

The *"Systems Transformation Model"*[123] is a very different growth model from the first one since it involves an "extension to specific or general obligations that are beyond the bounds of the original treaty obligations, either geographically or functionally," and lead to an important qualitative change in the scope and institutional capacities of the system; this "requires an entirely new constitutive bargaining process among the member states, entailing substantial goal redefinition among the national political actors."[124] The exercise of national leadership by the ruling élites, then, constitutes one of the most crucial factors of success.

Lindberg's distinction between these two growth models is fundamental since it enables him to refute the first model of Haas, who tends to assimilate these two processes, which are both considered to be the results of the "expansive logic of sectoral integration," whereas the object of Lindberg's analysis is to prove that the spill-over has played only a very limited role in the passage of the ECSC to the EEC: a "qualitative leap" has been made, setting in motion a new process.

While these two growth models have been very important in the history of the Community, Lindberg sees the future basically in terms of equilibrium, this model[125] showing how a given level of integration can be maintained in time and despite the tensions to which the system is subjected. In a sector which enjoys equilibrium it is the "adjustment negotiation" within the established rules which predominates, embracing only a limited category of actors who are concerned primarily with maintaining the existing level of integration and not with its growth. According to Lindberg, this situation involves elements of luck and risk. The lasting institutionalization and regularization inherent in the situation are, in fact, vital elements of the support and legitimization which benefit the system; but if the pressure of conservative forces grows too strong, there is a risk that this will lead to the stagnation of the system unless a serious crisis[126] incites the actors to find a new equilibrium through a further progression of functional integration along the lines of the forward linkage model.

The empirical analysis of these different models leads Lindberg to conclude that a "healthy" community system should include certain sectors in a state of equilibrium accompanied by efforts to bring about incremental growth and transformation of the system undertaken in a relatively small number of areas simultaneously.

In fact, he believes that the Community, after having passed through an initial phase of growth, has now entered a second phase in which the proportion of sectors in equilibrium will increase and in which, contrary to the predictions of the neofunctionalists, the successes of integration will impede its growth because of the conservative forces they engender.

He is also conscious of the limitations of his growth model, since it assumes that certain conditions or certain factors, considered as parameters, are established or constant, and since, in particular, it does not indicate the fundamental causes of the variations in the flow of demands and leadership. Now, under the influence of the persistence of a community in equilibrium, these parameters are destined to evolve or transform themselves in an unpredictable manner. Lindberg concludes, therefore, that his model is insufficient to assess problems raised by this new type of system, and he foresees the necessity of complementary approaches in order that progress in integration theory shall continue.

This inevitably brief survey of the work of Lindberg has, nonetheless, enabled us to assess the evolution of his ideas from the time when he was a student of Haas, and to draw attention to his basic contribution to the new trends in theoretical research into European integration.

CONCLUSION

Several conclusions emerge from this analysis of the main theories of European integration. First, the attempt at European organization is considered by the specialists to be the most advanced form of integration and the experimental field most advantageous for the testing of general integration models and theories. This explains why, in the early days, there was a proliferation of theses and interpretations, sometimes in competition with each other, of a phenomenon which was not appreciated in terms of its total reality but in relation to certain of its components, and which was based on different premises and definitions.

The evolution of the Community itself beyond the categories implicitly accepted at the outset, and its development as "a body of quasi-permanent institutions distinct from a progression towards federalism,"[127] has led the most recent authors to abandon these partial views in favor of research into a more general conceptual schema capable of taking into account the complexity of the phenomenon and its dynamics.

The systemic analysis used in the latest studies claims to fill this need, insofar as it is presented as the combination of an analytical technique and a series of theoretical propositions. It tries, in fact, to identify the basic processes, to isolate the variables deemed to be the most significant and to formulate hypotheses, which can be verified empirically, about the correlations which necessarily unite them.

On the basis of this approach, current research work seems to be directed not so much toward the formulation—based on the European case—of a general theory of integration but toward the construction of "models." These "models" are considered as structures within which theories can be related to each other, as a framework capable of assembling new data and as stages in in the development of a systematic theory.

Notes:

[1] K. Kaiser, "L'Europe des Savants, European Integration, and the Social Sciences," *Journal of Common Market Studies* 4 (1), October 1966, pp. 36–46.

[2] S. Hoffmann, "Theory and International Relations," in J. N. Rosenau (ed.), *International Politics and Foreign Policy: A Reader in Research and Theory*, New York, Free Press, 1969, p. 30.

[3] K. W. Deutsch, *Political Community at the International Level: Problems of Definition and Measurement*, New York, Doubleday and Co., 1954.

[4] K. W. Deutsch, et al., *Political Community and the North Atlantic Area: International Organization in the Light of Historical Experience*, Princeton, N.J., Princeton University Press, 1957.

[5] K. W. Deutsch, *Political Community and the North Atlantic Area . . .*, p. 5.

[6] Deutsch thus points out that the movement toward integration demands a surplus of capabilities in relation to loads since the latter, by engaging the capacity of attention or decision of governments, leads to a decline in their aptitude to cooperate. Integration is thus seen as a "work of expansion and not as a combination of fears and weaknesses."

[7] S. Hoffmann, "Vers l'étude systématique des mouvements d'intégration internationale," *Revue française de science politique*, 9 (2), June 1959, p. 476.

[8] K. W. Deutsch, *Nationalism and Social Communications: An Inquiry Into the Foundations of Nationality*, New York, John Wiley. London, Chapman and Hall, 1953.

[9] K. W. Deutsch, *The Nerves of Government: Models of Political Communications and Control*, New York, Free Press, 1963.

[10] K. W. Deutsch, "The Impact of Communications Upon International Relations Theory," in Abdul A. Saïd (ed.), *Theory of International Relations: The Crisis of Relevance*, Englewood Cliffs, N.J., Prentice-Hall, Inc., 1968.

[11] K. W. Deutsch, "Communication Theory and Political Integration," in P. Jacob and J. V. Toscano, (eds.), *The Integration of Political Communities*, New York, Philadelphia, J. B. Lippincott, 1964.

[12] K. W. Deutsch, *Arms Control and the Atlantic Alliance: Europe Faces Coming Policy Decisions*, New York, John Wiley and Sons, 1967. K. W. Deutsch et al., *France, Germany and the Western Alliance: A Study of Elite Attitudes on European Integration and World Politics*, New York, C. Scribner's and Sons, 1967.

[13] Cf. also a summary of these works: K. W. Deutsch, "Effort d'intégration dans le complexe de la politique européenne," in D. Sidjanski (ed.), *Méthodes quantitatives et intégration européenne*, Geneva, Institut universitaire d'études européennes, 1970. The text appeared earlier, entitled "Integration and Arms Control in the European Political Environment: A Summary Report," *American Political Science Review*, 60 (2), June 1966, pp. 354–65.

14 Cf. K. W. Deutsch, "Towards an Inventory of Basic Trends and Patterns in Comparative and International Politics,"*American Political Science Review*, 54 (1), March 1960, pp. 34–37.

15 K. W. Deutsch and R. Savage, "A Method for the Gross Analysis of Transaction Flows," *Econometrica*, 17 (3), July 1960, pp. 551–72.

16 K. W. Deutsch, *Arms Control and the Atlantic Alliance*, p. 20.

17 The other conclusions point out the unpopularity of national nuclear weapons, the persistence of the Atlantic link, the greater popularity for universalist solutions compared to regional solutions. Cf. P. Hassner, "De l'Arms Control aux S.A.L.T.," *Revue française de science politique*, 19 (6), December 1969, pp. 1266–71.

18 K. W. Deutsch, et al., *France, Germany and the Western Alliance*, p. 298.

19 Cf. especially K. W. Deutsch, *The Analysis of International Relations*, Englewood Cliffs, N.J., Prentice-Hall, Inc., 1968, p. 202; and "The Impact of Communications Upon International Relations Theory," in Abdul A. Saïd, (ed.), *op. cit.*, pp. 90–92.

20 K. W. Deutsch, *The Analysis of International Relations*, p. 188.

21 *Ibid.*, p. 192.

22 *Ibid.*, p. 202.

23 K. W. Deutsch, *Nationalism and Social Communication*, pp. 60–67.

24 Cf., for example, D. J. Singer, "Le théoricien incomplet ou la perspective sans l'évidence," pp. 6–33 in D. Sidjanski, (ed.), *op. cit.* Cf. also D. J. Singer, (ed.), *Quantitative International Politics; Insights and Evidence*, New York, Free Press, 1968.

25 B. Russett, for example, is not concerned with European integration directly but from the viewpoint of regional studies. His researches are devoted to an attempt to identify regions within the international system by the use of various data, and not by the geographical criteria alone. Cf. especially *International Regions and the International System*, Chicago, Rand McNally, 1967. The empirical research work of Russett is in line with the hypotheses and methods of Deutsch, which he has, in fact, applied, with several additions, to Anglo–American relations in an earlier work: *Community and Contention: Britain and America in the Twentieth Century*, Cambridge, Mass., M.I.T. Press, 1963.

26 D. Puchala, *International Political Community Formation in Western Europe: Progress and Prospects*, unpublished Ph.D. dissertation, Yale University, 1966.

27 H. Alker and D. Puchala, "Trends in Economic Partnership: the North Atlantic Area 1928–1963," in D. Singer, (ed.), *op. cit.*, p. 288.

28 Other suggested indicators are: amount of investments, attitudes of the masses and élite groups, existence of supranational political authorities, etc.

29 H. Alker and D. Puchala, in D. Singer (ed.), *op. cit.*, p. 289.

30 Cf. *infra* the recent works of D. Puchala.

31 S. Hoffmann, "Obstinate or Obsolete? The Fate of the Nation-state and the Case of Western Europe," *Daedalus*, 95 (3), Summer 1966, pp. 862–915.

[32] S. Hoffmann, "Vers l'étude systématique des mouvements d'intégration régionale," *art. cit.*, p. 479.

[33] R. Inglehart, "La fin de l'intégration européenne?" in D. Sidjanski, (ed.), *op. cit.*, p. 87.

[34] For a discussion of this interpretation by R. Inglehart of the AR index, see D. Handley, "Mesure de l'intégration dans la Communauté européenne, 1936–1968. Exemple de l'indice d'acceptation relative," in D. Sidjanski (ed.), *op. cit.*, pp. 95–118. In this article, D. Handley elaborates on the technique developed by Deutsch by working out methods of using statistical data for establishing the index. In addition, he extends the calculations of this index in the Common Market for the period 1963–68 by highlighting commercial transactions.

[35] R. Inglehart, "The New Europeans: Inward or Outward Looking?" *International Organization*, 24 (1), Winter 1970, pp. 129–39; and "Cognitive Mobilization and European Identity," *Comparative Politics*, 3 (1), October 1970, pp. 45–70.

[36] R. Inglehart, "La fin de l'intégration européenne?" *op. cit.*, p. 87.

[37] Cf. *infra* L. Lindberg in particular.

[38] R. Inglehart, "Trends and Non-trends in the Western Alliance: A Review," *Journal of Conflict Resolution*, 12 (1), March 1968, pp. 126–27.

[39] W. Fisher, "An Analysis of the Deutsch Social-causal Paradigm of Political Integration," *International Organization*, 23 (2), Spring 1969, pp. 254–90.

[40] E. Haas, *The Uniting of Europe: Political, Social and Economic Forces, 1950–1957*, Stanford, Calif., Stanford University Press, 1968.

[41] M. Banks, "Systems Analysis and the Study of Regions," *International Studies Quarterly*, 13 (4), December 1969, p. 355.

[42] E. Haas, "The Challenge of Regionalism," *International Organization*, 12 (4), Autumn 1958, pp. 440–58.

[43] E. Haas, *The Uniting of Europe*, p. xviii.

[44] "Increment" is defined as follows in *Littré* (French dictionary) : "An ancient term for the calculation of fluxions or differential calculus. The infinitely small quantity, from which a quantity grows."

[45] E. Haas, "The Uniting of Europe and the Uniting of Latin America," *Journal of Common Market Studies*, 5 (4), June 1967, p. 322.

[46] By groups, Haas means professional organizations, political parties and governments. See E. Haas, *The Uniting of Europe*, p. 15.

[47] E. Haas, "The Uniting of Europe and the Uniting of Latin America," *art. cit.*, p. 320.

[48] *Ibid.*, p. 323.

[49] E. Haas, "Technocracy, Pluralism and the New Europe," in S. Graubard, (ed.), *A New Europe?*, Boston, Houghton Mifflin Co., 1964.

[50] E. Haas, *The Uniting of Europe*, p. 7.

[51] E. Haas, "International Integration: The European and the Universal Process," *International Organization*, 15 (3), Summer 1961, pp. 366–92.

[52] E. Haas, *The Uniting of Europe*, p. 17.

53 *Ibid.*, p. xxiii.

54 E. Haas, "International Integration . . ." Haas describes the different agreements which can be reached at the end of negotiations.

55 E. Haas, *The Uniting of Europe*, chapter 8.

56 See L. N. Lindberg on this point, "Integration as a Source of Stress on the European Community System," *International Organization*, 20 (2), Spring 1966, pp. 233–65.

57 E. Haas, *The Uniting of Europe*, p. 5.

58 M. Banks, *art. cit.* See also P. Taylor, who considers Haas as a federalist in "The Concept of Community and the European Integration Process," *Journal of Common Market Studies*, 7 (2), December 1968, pp. 83–101.

59 L. N. Lindberg, *The Political Dynamics of Economic European Integration*, Stanford, Calif., Stanford University Press, 1963.

60 Lindberg enumerates four series of factors which condition the process: development of central institutions, "activation" of the process by elite groups, expansive, internal logic of the concrete areas of integration, and continuity of political aims of member states, excluding neither diversity of motivations nor conflicts of interests. *Ibid.*, pp. 8–12.

61 The author is referring here to the theses argued since 1960 by J. Schokking and N. Anderson, who foresee the possibility of the emergence in Europe of a "pluralist political structure, hitherto unknown . . . which might very well permit to a great extent the participating nations to retain their identity, while yet joined in the organizations that transcend nationality." J. J. Schokking, and N. Anderson, "Observations on the European Integration Process," *Journal of Conflict Resolution*, 4, 1960, pp. 385–410.

62 L. N. Lindberg, *The Political Dynamics of Economic European Integration*, p. 5.

63 *Ibid.*

64 *Ibid.*, p. 6.

65 Cf. the main part of L. N. Lindberg, *The Political Dynamics of Economic European Integration* and "Decision Making and Integration in the European Community," *International Organization*, 20 (1), Winter 1965, pp. 58–80.

66 In R. C. Macridis and B. E. Brown, (eds.), *Comparative Politics*, Homewood, Ill., Dorsey Press, 1961.

67 Cf. *infra.*

68 B. Balassa, *The Theory of Economic Integration*, London, G. Allen and Unwin, 1962; L. Krauss, *European Economic Integration and the United States*, Washington, D.C., Brookings Institution, 1968.

69 L. Krause, quoted by R. Hansen, "Regional Integration. Reflections on a Decade of Theoretical Efforts," *World Politics*, 11 (2), January 1969, pp. 254–55.

70 *Ibid.*, p. 254.

71 A. Marchal, *L'Europe solidaire: Les problèmes*, Paris, Cujas, 1970.

72 E. Haas, *The Uniting of Europe*, p. 299.

73 See E. Haas, "The Uniting of Europe and the Uniting of Latin America," *art. cit.*, p. 325.

74 S. Hoffmann, "Discord in Community: the North Atlantic Area as a Partial International System," *International Organization*, 17 (2), Spring 1963, p. 529.

75 *Ibid.*

76 *Ibid.*

77 E. Haas, "The Uniting of Europe . . ." p. 315.

78 E. Haas and P. Schmitter, "Economics and Differential Patterns of Political Integration: Projections About Unity in Latin America," *International Organization,* 18 (2), Spring 1964, p. 709.

79 *Ibid.*, pp. 709–10.

80 E. Haas, "The Uniting of Europe . . ." p. 328.

81 See the paradigm of Haas and Schmitter, "Economics and Differential Patterns. . . ."

82 *Ibid.*, p. 717.

83 E. Haas, "The Uniting of Europe . . ." pp. 329–30.

84 J. S. Nye, Jr., "Patterns and Catalysts in Regional Integration," *International Organization*, 19 (4), Autumn 1965, pp. 870–84.

85 A. Etzioni, "A Paradigm for the Study of Political Unification," *World Politics*, 15 (1), October 1962, p. 44; A. Etzioni, "The Epigenesis of Political Communities at the International Level," in J. Rosenau, (ed.), *International Politics and Foreign Policy: A Reader in Research and Theory*, New York Free Press, 1969, pp. 346–58.

86 J. S. Nye, Jr., *Comparing Integration Process: A Suggestion for a Revision of the Haas-Schmitter Paradigm*, Geneva, European Centre of the Carnegie Foundation. 1969. See comments of S. Bernard, "Réflexions sur l'état présent de la théorie de l'intégration régionale," report presented to the Eighth World Congress of the AISP, Munich, August 31–September 5, 1970. Draft manuscript, mimeo.

87 J. S. Nye, Jr., "Comparative Regional Integration: Concept and Measurement," *International Organization*, 22 (4), Autumn 1968, p. 858.

88 Cf. L. N. Lindberg and S. Scheingold, (eds.), "Regional Integration: Theory and Research," *International Organization*, 24 (4), Autumn 1970, pp. 607–1020. The collected contributions in this special number—published after this article was printed—confirm the direction of present research work and reveal, in fact, that a fairly wide agreement exists on this point between the authors (Preface, p. vii).

89 D. Puchala, "Patterns in West European Integration," report presented to the Congress of the American Political Science Association, Los Angeles, September 1970, p. 6.

90 D. Puchala, "The Pattern of Contemporary Regional Integration," *International Studies Quarterly*, 12 (1), March 1968.

91 *Ibid.*, p. 47.

92 Cf. the relationship, underlined by D. Puchala himself, between his ideas and those of J. Nye on the way to study integration. D. Puchala, "Integration and Disintegration in Franco-German Relations, 1954–1965," *International Organization*, 24 (2), Spring 1970, p. 183. Although they extend beyond the

setting of European integration, the studies of Nye are, in fact, along the same lines. Cf., especially J. Nye, "Comparative Regional Integration: Concept and Measurement," *International Organization*, 22 (4), Autumn 1968, pp. 855–80.

93 D. Puchala, "The Pattern of Contemporary Regional Integration."

94 *Ibid.*, p. 59.

95 In particular by A. Etzioni, *Political Unification*, New York, Holt Rinehart and Winston, 1965, pp. 58–59.

96 D. Puchala, "International Transactions and Regional Integration," *International Organization*, 24 (4), Autumn 1970, pp. 732–63.

97 R. Merritt and D. Puchala, *Western European Perspectives on International Affairs*, New York, Praeger, 1968; D. Puchala, "The Common Market and Political Federation in Western European Public Opinion," *International Studies Quarterly*, 24 (1), March 1970, pp. 32–60.

98 D. Puchala, "International Transactions and Regional Integration," pp. 736–37.

99 D. Puchala, "Integration and Disintegration in Franco-German Relations," pp. 191–98.

100 D. Puchala, "Patterns in West European Integration," pp. 43–46.

101 L. N. Lindberg, "The European Community as a Political System. Notes Toward the Construction of a Model," *Journal of Common Market Studies*, 5 (4), June 1967, pp. 344–87.

102 Cf. D. Easton, *A Framework for Political Analysis*, Englewood Cliffs, N.J., Prentice-Hall, Inc., 1965, xvi–143 pp.; and his *A Systems Analysis of Political Life*, New York, John Wiley and Sons, Inc., 1965.

103 L. N. Lindberg, "The European Community as a Political System," p. 346.

104 *Ibid.*, p. 349.

105 L. N. Lindberg and S. A. Scheingold, *Europe's Would-be Polity: Patterns of Change in the European Community*, Englewood Cliffs, N.J., Prentice-Hall, Inc., 1970, vi–314 pp.

106 An early version of the progress of his research on this point is included in *Europe as a Political System: Measuring Political Integration*, unpublished manuscript, Center for International Affairs, Harvard University, April 1967. For a more detailed and up-to-date exposition of this aspect of the author's research work, cf. L. N. Lindberg, "Political Integration as a Multidimensional Phenomenon Requiring Multivariate Measurement," *International Organization*, 24 (4), Autumn 1970, pp. 649–731.

107 L. N. Lindberg, "The European Community as a Political System," pp. 352–73.

108 L. N. Lindberg and S. A. Scheingold, *Europe's Would-be Polity*, p. 98.

109 Cf. the graph showing the main setbacks and successes in Community negotiations 1952–68, *ibid.*, p. 104.

110 For the study of the crises inherent in the system cf. L. N. Lindberg, "Integration as a Source of Stress on the European Community System," *International Organization*, 20 (2), Spring 1966, pp. 233–63. The author takes the 1965 crisis as an example of how "the struggle over the form and content

of structures and procedures by virtue of which obligatory decisions are made" constitutes a "permanent source of tension" for the system.

111 E. Haas and P. Schmitter, "Economics and Differential Patterns of Political Integration . . ."

112 L. N. Lindberg and S. A. Scheingold, *Europe's Would-be Polity*, p. 39.

113 It is interesting to note that the most recent work of R. Inglehart on the role of public opinion in the integration process also makes use of Easton's analysis framework: the relationship between the attitudes of public opinion and decision-making is, in fact, presented in terms of a feedback model (retroactive effects linking the outputs of the system to the societal input). Cf. R. Inglehart, "Public Opinion and Regional Integration," *International Organization*, 24 (4), Autumn 1970, pp. 764–96.

114 L. N. Lindberg and S. A. Scheingold, *Europe's Would-be Polity*, p. 42.

115 *Ibid.*, p. 123. Lindberg does not accept, however, Haas's conclusions on the superiority of the "incremental-economic" actors.

116 For a more detailed discussion of the flow of demands and the presentation of certain suggestions aiming to measure it, cf. Lindberg, *Europe as a Political System: Measuring Political Integration*, unpublished manuscript (cf. *supra*, note 106). See also L. N. Lindberg, "Political Integration as a Multidimensional Phenomenon . . ." pp. 679–82.

117 L. N. Lindberg and S. A. Scheingold, *Europe's Would-be Polity*, pp. 130–31.

118 *Ibid.*, p. 117.

119 *Ibid.*, p. 119.

120 *Ibid.*, p. 120. The feedback concept is deliberately used here with far greater restraint than in the work of Easton.

121 L. N. Lindberg, "The European Community as a Political System," p. 350.

122 Each model is illustrated here by a double case study presenting it from the two aspects of success and failure. In the case of forward linkage, the results gained in the area of common agricultural policy are off-set by the setback encountered in the transport policy, qualified as output failure.

123 Cases of successful transformation are the treaties instituting the EEC and Euratom; examples of failures are the EDC Plan, the negotiations on the Fouchet Plan, and the entry of Great Britain into the Common Market.

124 L. N. Lindberg and S. A. Scheingold, *Europe's Would-be Polity*, p. 137.

125 Examples chosen to illustrate the success of this equilibrium model, or, on the other hand, the regression of the system (spill-back), are the achievement of the customs union and the crisis in the coal-mining area respectively.

126 For a presentation of the neo-functionalist theory of the crises of European integration, their causes and effects, cf. G. Zellentin, "Krisen der europäischen Integration, Ursachen und Wirkungen," *Integration, Vierteljahreshefte zur Europaforschung*, No. 1, 1970, pp. 20–37.

127 L. N. Lindberg, "The European Community as a Political System," p. 344.

THE EUROPEAN ECONOMIC COMMUNITY AND THE 1965 CRISIS
BY FRANÇOISE DE LA SERRE

The "empty chair" crisis of June 1965–January 1966, provoked by French President Charles de Gaulle, was the most serious threat to its continued existence that the EEC has faced. The French political scientist Françoise de la Serre not only reconstitutes the day-to-day struggles that paralyzed the Community for seven months but assesses the broader significance for the future pattern of European diplomacy of the crisis which, in her view, was caused by the existence of a partially integrated Community of European states. This chapter was originally published as an article, "La Communauté économique européenne et la crise de 1965," in Revue Française de Science Politique, Vol. XXI (2), April 1971, pp. 402–20. It is republished here by permission of the journal. The translation is by Helen Baz.

While international relations offer numerous examples of conflicts arising between states, the solution to which is sought within regional organizations, the crisis which took place in 1965 within the Common Market developed by an inverse process: it drew its origins, in fact, from the very existence and development of the Community organization, and was partially resolved outside the organization. After serving, to begin with, as the pretext and framework of the conflict setting France against her fellow-members and the Commission, at a later stage, the Community system became, to a certain extent, what was at stake.

This article does not set out to describe in detail the development of the crisis which occurred within the Common Market on June 30, 1965, and which was resolved, at least formally, by the Luxembourg agreements on January 30, 1966.[1] The crisis is examined here in terms of a study of French policy from April 1965 to January 1966, and it has two aims in mind. First, to try to determine whether the French attitude toward the community organization was "an important exercise in power politics,"[2] at what level, with what objectives, and with what immediate results. Second, to establish, on the basis of this particular example and from these earlier conclusions, a number of hypotheses concerning the role played by the particular type of international organization represented by the EEC in the organization of relations between its member countries and search for solutions to the conflicts arising among them.

A LIMITED EXERCISE IN POWER POLITICS

In agreement with quite a few other observers, we recognize, *a priori*, that the aim of the French government in June 1965 was not to withdraw from the Common Market, nor to destroy it, but to make use of the Community mechanisms to futher its own interests and objectives. Leon Lindberg, in this respect, points out that "if France withdrew or otherwise caused the total collapse of the system, France would forego its major lever of intervention in and possible disruption of its partners' internal affairs and its chief source of influence over its partners' policies towards the United States, the Soviet Union and Eastern Europe. If the European Community were to founder, West Germany, Italy, Benelux, as indeed the United Kingdom itself, would have no alternative to an 'Atlantic solution.' . . . Furthermore, a 'break' would be very costly to French industry and agriculture alike."[3] It is in this perspective that we will examine the process of the crisis which began on June 30, 1965.

The Origins of the Crisis

The initial cause of the breakdown which occurred in Brussels on June 30, 1965, arose from problems encountered in the negotiation of a technical question concerning the financing of the Common Agricultural Policy. The first agreement among the six partners of the Common Market on a common agricultural policy had, in fact, been reached on January 14, 1962, when they decided on the organization of various markets and established financing regulations which defined the conditions of the progressive take-over of agricultural expenditure by the Community. The procedure for this Community financing had been agreed, in the first place, for the period up to June 30, 1965, and secondly, for the period extending beyond the transition period, that is, after January 1, 1970. In the case of the first period, Community financing was guaranteed by contributions from member states, in the second period by paying into the Community fund the total amount of agricultural levies. When the Mansholt Plan was adopted in December 1964 (a common price for cereals on July 1, 1967, and community appropriation of levies), the Six had undertaken, on the insistence of France in particular, to reach an agreement before June 30, 1965, on the adoption of a financing regulation for the end of the transition period (1965–70), which was not covered by the provisions already laid down. The Commission was invited to submit proposals to the Council on this issue.

By seeking to complete the implementation of the Common Agricultural Policy in this way, the objective of the French government was to further its most basic interests, since the Community appropriation of agricultural levies enshrined the principles of preference and Community responsibility, to which it attached the utmost importance.

As M. Couve de Murville was to say: "The French government was not prepared, bearing in mind the important role played by agriculture in our economy, to allow itself to be drawn into fixing farm price-rises without knowing how the agricultural policy was to be financed."[4]

On this particular issue, then, the French government appeared in the role of "applicant," from which position it was attempting to demand a few gestures of European goodwill in return for French interests being satisfied. The forthcoming passage to the third stage of the Rome Treaty (when certain decisions would be passed by a majority), the imminent revision of the consecutive treaties by the fusion of their Executives, the pressure exerted by certain countries in favor of extending the powers of the European Parliament in the name of a "democratization" of the Community—all these factors probably spurred on the Commission to submit certain proposals to the Council of Ministers, which were presented as "indivisible," extending far beyond the single technical problem of agricultural financing, and which, they maintained, lay within the logic of French demands but implied a revision of the Treaty.

Without going into detail about the complex arrangements proposed by the Commission, its plan can be presented in three sections. The first concerns the modification and completion of the financing regulation, which had been asked for by the Council of Ministers, but this was accompanied by two other related texts of far-reaching political implications. The latter suggested bringing forward to July 1, 1967, the total elimination of customs duties on industrial products and putting into force the common external tariff, and paying into the European Fund, not only the agricultural levies, but also the product of the customs duties. The proposals ended by suggesting that the Commission should have its "own resources," in other words, a real European budget. These resources, earmarked in particular for the financing of exports of surplus products and for the support of agricultural investments, would not come within the jurisdiction of national parliaments. It would, therefore, have to come under the control of the European Parliament, whose powers would thus be considerably increased, as would—by a subtle game of "shuttle diplomacy"—the powers of the Commission.[5] Was the French government, in return for a settlement of the financing regulation, whose importance has already been mentioned, prepared to accept from 1967 onward this type of federal budget controlled by the European Parliament, and to commit itself to the enmeshment of supranationality? The declarations of General de Gaulle and his ministers, whether before or immediately following the publication of the Commission's report, leave little room for doubt as to the intentions of the French government, since they reject any form of integration at whatever level or within whatever framework it might be. M. Couve de Murville, for example, stated in the National Assembly on May 20: "Our partners are indulging in wishful thinking by putting forward proposals which they know France will not accept." In such a situation, which had brought to the surface the contradictions existing between the pursuit of Community progress and French demands for independence, what were the objectives of the French government? What direction did their policy take throughout this period?

French Strategy and Tactics

Up to June 30, 1965, the main objective of the French government was still to secure the agricultural financing regulation, although this was not matched by the slightest concession concerning the Community's "own resources" and of their control by the European Parliament. By defending this position, the French government confirmed that it was still firmly committed to the undertakings agreed to in 1962 and 1964, under the terms of which, according to the French, only the first part of the Commission's proposals, concerning the financial regulation, should be examined. The French maintained that the Commission, by putting forward other proposals, had gone well beyond the mandate it had been given by the Council of Ministers. Moreover, still referring to the undertakings agreed to, the French argument pointed out the inflexible nature of the timetable and the necessity to conclude the settlement before July 1, 1965.

The French government took various initiatives, based on this position, to ensure the success of its objectives. First of all, it set out to evaluate the degree of support which its partners were prepared to give to the whole of the Commission's plan and to play on the differences existing between them. Indeed, although the Five seemed willing to accept the global and indivisible nature of the proposals and, therefore, to negotiate the different points, it soon became clear that serious reservations were emerging: German and, particularly, Italian misgivings about the financing clauses and the duration of the agricultural regulation, doubts on the part of the Netherlands about handing over the product of the customs duties to the Commission, and a more or less open hostility by the German government to a decrease in the powers of the Council of Ministers in favor of the Commission and the European Parliament.

This situation encouraged the French government to seek, with West Germany, not a firm agreement, hampered by the serious differences existing between the two countries on the majority of international problems, but at least some kind of package deal.[6] They might, on the one hand, gain support for the financing regulation which France was hoping for in return for supporting West German demands in respect to the industrial Common Market and the Kennedy Round. On the other hand, General de Gaulle unequivocally linked the acceptance of the Common Agricultural Policy with the problem of European political union and especially with the calling of a summit conference which Chancellor Erhard was so eager to bring about. At the time of the Rambouillet talks in January 1965, Erhard had even managed to obtain an agreement in principle from the French President on this point. The communiqué published on March 31 after the meeting of the Council of Ministers contains a significant reference to this issue. Referring to the adjournment—at the request of the French—of the conference of foreign ministers, which was to have taken place on May 10 in Venice in order to prepare for this European summit, M. Peyrefitte stated, in particular: "The French position has not changed since the initiative taken on this matter in 1960–61 and since the talks between General de Gaulle and Chancellor Erhard last January. It is important that these talks should be continued in order to reach an agreement, if only because the Common Market itself could not survive in the long-term without close political cooperation among its members. A conference of heads of state and governments would, therefore, be welcomed as soon as the important discussions going on in Brussels at present, especially concerning agriculture, are brought to a satisfactory conclusion, which is expected on June 30."

It is within this setting that the meeting between Erhard and de Gaulle took place in Bonn on June 11 and 12, which apparently did not result in any formal commitment by either of them. Was this failure to reach agreement the reason for the radical change in French tactics? On June 15, at the meeting of the Council of Ministers of the EEC, M. Couve de Murville proposed a new basis for discussion. France declared that she was ready to defer until 1970 the Community allocations of levies agreed for July 1, 1967. On this date the national subsidies for the export of products subject to the single-price system would be refunded by the Common Fund, but the Fund would continue to be fed by national contributions. Since the Common Market would, therefore, not possess its "own resources," the problem of their control by the European Parliament would no longer arise. The only remaining question would be the method of calculating the "keys" regulating members' contributions to the Fund from July 1, 1965. The aim of these proposals was clearly to divest the June 30 agreement of its political substance at the price of a temporary renunciation of the considerable advantages to be gained by France from the Mansholt Plan. While it is difficult to isolate the role of pure tactics within this initiative, it does highlight the hierarchy of objectives pursued by the French government: the settlement of the financing regulation gives way, when necessary, to the struggle against supranationalism.

A final attempt to establish the creation of a Franco–German front took place on June 22 in the Lahr–Wormser talks, and agreement seemed to have been reached on the following points: the simultaneous nature of the agricultural Common Market and the Customs Union, allocation of agricultural levies to the Commission on January 1, 1970, re-examination of the problem of the appropriation of customs duties, agreement in principle on the limited and progressive extension of powers of the European Parliament. It was on the basis of these positions and those defended by the Italian–Dutch coalition on the side of the Commission that the last act of the negotiations took place from June 28 to June 30.

We do not intend to give a detailed analysis of these negotiations here, but merely to pick out the main lines of the French position. Although, to begin with, France was confronted with a relatively united front which accepted the global nature of the Commission's proposals (Netherlands–Italy), and a prolongation of the talks beyond June 30 (the Five), it was soon to realize once more that differences of opinion existed among its partners concerning the problem of the Community's "own resources" and their control by the European Parliament. These disagreements among its fellow-members and its own favorable interpretation of the Lahr–Wormser talks seemed to justify France concentrating its efforts on the negotiation of a financing regulation only, an area in which it was in fundamental opposition to Italy.

It seems, however, that this desire to settle the financing regulation without committing France at all, even in principle, to any of the other proposals, its refusal to prolong the negotiations beyond June 30, the threats about the consequences of failure to France, were seen by the German delegation as being contrary to the Lahr–Wormser agreement. Herr Schroeder gave his own interpretation of this agreement in a "tough" speech in which he underlined the global nature of the proposals of the Commission, and reminded his partners that the Council had not always kept to the timetable which had been fixed on past occasions. Above all, he moved even further away from the French position by pointing out that a resolution had been passed unanimously that very afternoon of June 30 by the Bundestag, which called for a strengthening of the powers of the European Parliament.

This switching of allegiance by West Germany, whom General de Gaulle was later to hold as one of those responsible for the crisis, rendered impossible from then on both the success of French initiatives and the tireless efforts at conciliation throughout the negotiations on the part of Belgium and Luxembourg. The French delegation drew the logical conclusions from the situation by suspending the debate and by refusing to join in a "marathon" which, in any case, was unlikely to occur in the absence of alternative proposals put forward by the Commission.

M. Couve de Murville, when he pointed out, on leaving the meeting of the Council of Ministers, "the absence of any political willingness to reach an agreement," summed up clearly the root of the problem. The debate had, in fact, revealed, over and above the defense of legitimate national interests, the opposition of France's fellow-members to a policy of ultimatum and to attempts at domination which had been pursued repeatedly, and notably taken to its extreme at the time of the 1963 negotiations with Great Britain.

What conclusions can be drawn from the preceding developments as to French policy in the Common Market up to June 30, 1965? French moves, directed toward obtaining a financing regulation, which it considered as a solemn obligation of the Community, were in more or less direct opposition to the aims of the Commission and to the interests and convictions of its partners; it had tried to induce them to agree to French terms by tactics combining the use of pressure, bargaining, the ultimatum, similar to methods used during previous negotiations and which, up to then, had been successful. Yet this first round of the contest had apparently ended in deadlock, since France, once convinced that the financing regulation could not be obtained without making concessions in other areas, seemed to have resigned itself to a breakdown of negotiations. While the latter can be shown to be based on legal differences, it does bring to light, however, the opposition of the Five to the demands and methods of French diplomacy. The fact that the break had probably been deliberate, which is borne out by the haste with which M. Couve de Murville suspended the debate and by his refusal to join in any "marathon," does not necessarily modify this conclusion at this stage of the analysis.

June 30, however, was merely the date which separated two phases of the same conflict. This first attempt to "exercise power," directed toward the adoption of the agricultural regulation without conceding any institutional modifications, was followed by a determination to exploit the crisis and to ensure that the French viewpoint should prevail in the fundamental area concerning the nature and functioning of community institutions. By pursuing a policy of the "empty chair" and by seeking to paralyze the Common Market, General de Gaulle seemed "to be weighing up the advantages of an action which, using the Community as a hostage, would break down any resistance to his grand design."[7]

THE COMMUNITY SYSTEM PUT IN JEOPARDY AGAIN
The True Dimensions of the Conflict

On July 1, the day after the breakdown of negotiations, the French government announced, at the close of the meeting of the Council of Ministers, "that it had decided, as far as it is concerned, to draw the legal, economic and political consequences of the situation which has just been created."[8] On July 7, the nature of the measures decided upon by the French government were made public. First, ministers would no longer participate in any meetings connected with the Six until further notice, whether within the framework of the Common Market, the ECSC, or Euratom.[9] Futhermore, the French representative with the European Communities was "invited" to return to Paris. Finally, French civil servants would no longer take part in meetings which could lead to new Community decisions. This boycott, which blocked any further development of the Common Market and which, contrary to the terms of the Treaty—members having undertaken not to impede the efficient functioning of the Communities—left the other member countries and the Commission in no doubt whatsoever as to the serious intentions of the French government. Although France's true objectives were still not made clear despite intensive diplomatic activity pursued on a number of occasions—in particular, at the Paris meeting of the NATO Council on July 12—two characteristics seem to epitomize the French position at this stage of the crisis, which emerged, in particular, from the speech given by M. Pompidou on July 27. First, the responsibility for the conflict continued to be placed on the Five, especially Italy, and the Commission, which was, once again, accused of having exceeded its powers.[10] Second, France did not appear to be anxious to reopen negotiations, even on the single problem of the agricultural financing regulation. The failure to agree on this particular issue had been given on July 1 by M. Couve de Murville as the cause of the breakdown, but this question now no longer seemed to be a central issue for the French government. Nor did the Prime Minister allude, in his speech, to the new proposals put forward several days earlier, on July 22, in a memorandum from the Commission and which, nevertheless, went a very long way to satisfying French demands. The memorandum, in fact, proposed the simultaneous implementation of the agricultural and industrial Common Market on July 1, 1967, and retained the ambitious timetable adopted in June by the Ministers of Agriculture for the fixing of farm prices. In addition, it was suggested that the Community should not acquire its "own resources" until January 1, 1970. In the meantime, the

Commission proposed—trying to meet some of the demands of the Italians—that the fixing of the scale of payments to be fed into the agricultural fund for the coming four and a half years should be in accordance with French demands made in June. Moreover, the thorny question of the European Parliament was not raised except to defer it to a later examination. Finally, although the necessity for Community progress in other areas was mentioned, following the wishes of the West Germans in particular, this was not explicitly linked to the problem of the agricultural financing regulation.

The French government's failure to react to these new proposals, even though they were stripped of any political implications, made it clear that from then on, as far as France was concerned, the problem lay elsewhere.

The firm stand of the French, combined with official silence at the highest levels, was probably due in part to its desire to embarrass its partners and to put to the test the coalition of June 30, which Paris believed to be accidental, and within which Belgium and Luxembourg were clearly anxious to bring about a compromise with France. Indeed, it was with some reluctance that these two countries agreed to the meeting of the Council of the ECSC on July 13 and to that of the EEC Council on July 26. By and large, the Five, throughout the summer, seemed anxious to maintain the best possible functioning of Community mechanisms, while at the same time taking care to avoid any actions which would make it more difficult for France to return to the negotiating table.

It was not until after General de Gaulle's press conference on September 9, however, that the preconditions for this return and the profound significance, the true dimensions, which the head of the French state was determined to attribute to the crisis, clearly emerged. The first sentence of his statement was explicit in this respect. "What happened in Brussels on June 30 in connection with the agricultural financing regulation highlighted, not only the persistent reluctance of the majority of our partners to bring agriculture within the scope of the Common Market, but also certain mistakes or ambiguities of principle in the Treaties setting up the economic union of the Six. That is why the crisis was, sooner or later, inevitable." While the importance of the agricultural regulation to the French economy (demands for an "equitable" Community), and the non-respect of the other partners for undertakings made on this matter, continued to be emphasized, General de Gaulle also denounced the initiatives taken by the Commission in this area "which aim to turn this institution into a great independent financial power." Furthermore, criticisms of the actions of the Commission on this particular issue were accompanied by a more fundamental attack on the institution itself, as constituted in the Treaty, and on various other provisions in the Treaty mainly concerned with the majority vote. After having pointed out, first of all, that the Treaties setting up the ECSC, Euratom, and the Common Market "took into consideration the demands of others first and foremost," General de Gaulle attacked this "executive figuration . . . independent of the states . . . destined to tread on French democracy in the settlement of problems which control the very existence of our country." In fact, General de Gaulle believed that "no important issues arising at present in the organization, and later in the functioning of the Common Market, should be decided and implemented *a fortiori,* except by the responsible public powers in the six states, in other words by the governments controlled by parliaments." This demand, moreover, conformed to the French plan for "an organized cooperation between states evolving, no doubt, towards a confederation," but did not accord with the provisions of the Treaty, which sought, from January 1, 1966, to extend the majority vote to the Council of Ministers, whereas, from this same date, the proposals of the Commission could not be amended except by a unanimous vote. "France would be exposed to the possibility of being overruled in any economic, social and even sometimes political matters."[11] In conclusion, General de Gaulle announced that France intended to reopen negotiations in

Brussels, after discussions with other governments, "as soon as agriculture is brought fully within the scope of the Common Market, and as soon as people are ready to have done with the pretensions which ill-founded, Utopian myths raise up against common sense and reality."[12]

Thus, General de Gaulle had launched a fundamental attack on the Community method and on the provisions of the Rome Treaty which sought to turn the Common Market into something other than a classical international organization. With the aim of removing any supranational features from the European structure, he tried to obtain, by an inter-governmental agreement, a reduction in the powers of the Commission and to safeguard national independence by retaining the right of veto.

For General de Gaulle, the veto was vital at a time when developments in economic integration were in danger of restricting national freedom of action in the political field, since no agreement existed among fellow-members on the major issues of foreign policy and defense, which was the case in 1965. As Miriam Camps has pointed out: "If the other members of the Community would not accept the French concept of Europe, France must have independence of action. If France's partners had shared General de Gaulle's vision of Europe and had been prepared to accept the French view of what foreign and defense policies the Europe of the Six should follow there would doubtless have been no crisis."[13]

The speech given by M. Couve de Murville on October 20 in the National Assembly made the connection between the crisis and the lack of consensus among the Six on the political level quite explicit: "There is no doubt that economic Europe is in a state of crisis largely because political agreement did not follow. I repeat: because political agreement did not follow. If the political climate had been different among the Six of the Common Market, it would have been difficult to imagine that the discussion of problems which should have been resolved by July 1, 1965, would have ended in general disagreement, under such conditions that, in truth, there was never any real possibility, at any time, of entering into serious discussions of basic issues."

The Foreign Minister also continued the attacks, already made against the nonrespect for the undertakings on the agricultural regulation and against the Commission, which was accused of seeking to become "a real political authority, less and less controlled by the responsible governments." Above all, he made the position of the French government quite clear in calling for "a general revision in order to define the normal conditions for cooperation between the Six, since the functioning of the Brussels institution itself is at issue." The remainder, of the speech was devoted to a further rejection of supranationality, whether it took the form of a "judgment by the Commission" or of a "majority of governments excluding France." Finally, M. Couve de Murville repeated that "it was up to responsible governments and to them alone [to find a solution to the crisis], to debate it, and to come to an agreement."[14]

Were the partners of France prepared to agree to these demands in exchange for the return of France to the negotiating table and the end of the boycott of the Common Market?

Coalition and Compromise

It seemed that, on the contrary, the initial effect of this escalation of French demands was to strengthen the solidarity of the Five in defense of the Treaty. After their meeting on October 25, they issued an "urgent appeal to France to resume its place in the Community institutions," but this was coupled with a very firm declaration in which they "solemnly reaffirmed the necessity to carry on with the implementation of the Treaties of Paris and Rome, in accordance with the principles contained therein and with the aim of bringing about the progressive fusion of both their industrial and agricultural economies. . . . They believed that the solution to the problems facing the Communities must be found within the framework of the Treaties and their institutions."[15] Moreover, at this same meeting, the Five secretly agreed to act only as a collective body to forestall any possible maneuvers by the French to divide them. Finally, they proposed a compromise procedure to the French government, in the spirit of the plan put forward by M. Spaak in October, and invited France to join them in Brussels at a special meeting of the Council of Ministers, without the Commission, to discuss the general situation of the Communities.

This coalition, unprecedented in the history of the Community, led by West Germany, who was probably seeking as much to defend its own national interests by preventing the possibility of French hegemony in Europe as to preserve the community structure, left the French government in no doubt as to the size of the resistance to its demands. The French decision to reopen negotiations stemmed from this firm stand of the Five rather than from electoral considerations concerning the December presidential campaign of General de Gaulle. Indeed, at the end of November, M. Peyrefitte announced that "it seems likely that the foreign ministers will be meeting in the near future to discuss general problems," which probably implied that the French plan had been stopped. It is also probable that the offensive planned against NATO by General de Gaulle and the possibility of a rapprochement between the Five and Great Britain had persuaded him to settle the problem of the Common Market.[16]

The preparation for the negotiations was raised at various bilateral meetings, for France, although it had received a collective communiqué from the Five, refused to give any formal reply. Moreover, the Five were left in a state of uncertainty, up to the Luxembourg meeting on January 17 and 18, as to the precise formulation of the demands of the French government, which did not appear to be ready to relax the pressure imposed by its boycott of the Community. For example, France refused to vote, by the written procedure, the budgets of the Common Market and Euratom.

The demands put forward by M. Couve de Murville at the first Luxembourg meeting were aimed, on the one hand, at proscribing the principle of the majority vote and, on the other, at reducing the powers of the Commission. They were accompanied by the request for a timetable designed—once an agreement had been reached on the two preceding points—to speed up the community work in those areas in which France was concerned (agricultural regulation, new Commission, etc.). On the question of the majority vote, the French Minister no longer demanded a formal revision of the Treaty since the firm opposition of its partners to this proposal had been made quite clear, but he called for the signing of a kind of interpretative protocol re-establishing the principle of unanimity whenever a government believed its vital interests to be at stake. The problem of the powers of the Commission was dealt with in a ten-point document, the "decalogue." The main intention of this document was to ensure a certain "control over the Commission by the Council and to restrict its initiatives and its field of action, to impose a change of style in its external relations, to control more closely both its information policy and its administration of finances."[17] Since no agreement was reached at this first meeting between France and the Five, who continued to maintain their solid front, led by Herr Schroeder, the negotiators decided to adjourn their discussions until January 28. An agreement was reached at this second Luxembourg meeting on the night of January 29–30. We shall try to assess this agreement in terms of the initial demands of the French government.

In the first place, on the issue of the majority vote, the Five refused to give way to France and insisted on the principle of the majority vote laid down in the Treaty, while, for its part, the French government refused to modify its position. Finally, the conflicting attitudes of the partners led to the adoption of a formula which was more an agreement to disagree than a compromise. It contains, in fact, side by side, the two opposing views of the Five and of France, and the agreement to disagree, which would not prevent, however, according to them, the resumption of work by the Community.[18]

The agreement on the powers of the Commission was more

realistic, since the Six succeeded in drafting a kind of "code of good conduct," based on the French memorandum but which toned down considerably the French demands both in form and content. It was no longer a question of subjecting the Commission to some form of control by the Council, nor of restricting its right of initiative recognized by the Treaty, but merely of developing a closer collaboration between the Council and the Commission. As well as being asked to give governments prior notice of any important information, and to observe discretion in its public declarations, the Commission's freedom of action was restricted in respect of foreign relations, and its information policy and budgetary commitments were controlled.

Finally, a program of work was planned which was more favorable to the interests of the Five than the timetable proposed by M. Couve de Murville. It gave equal priority to the reopening of negotiations on the agricultural financing regulation and the examination of other issues such as that of the Kennedy Round. Furthermore, discussions on the membership of the Commission and the appointment of its president were given precedence over the depositing of the instruments of ratification of the fusion treaty (of Executives).

"France can succeed only by threatening to disrupt the whole Common Market," wrote M. Debré in September, after General de Gaulle's press conference.[19] Following the Luxembourg compromise, what had the French government gained as a result of the crisis? Had its demands been met by deliberately aggravating the conflict? Although the head of the French state affirmed this in his press conference on February 21, the success of this exercise in power politics seemed to be limited.

It is true that the terms of the agricultural financing regulation, over which the crisis of June 30 had arisen, seemed to have been favorable to French interests since the discussions were based on the second memorandum of the Commission, which was far closer to the French view.

Yet, on the institutional level, France was a long way off from obtaining the general revision of the Treaties which it had been calling for. The Five had refused to give up the principle of the majority vote, preferring to retain this as a lever to force the member countries to come to an agreement by becoming more flexible in their postures.

Nor did the text concerning the Commission formally change its powers laid down in the Treaty, and it recognized, furthermore, that the terms of cooperation between the council and the Commission should be established by mutual agreement of the two institutions. "The value of the Luxembourg agreements," it was said, "lay precisely in the fact that they had no juridical value, that the legal regulations and framework remained intact, and that they did not restrict in any way its future evolution and functioning."[20]

Nevertheless, although the Five refused to allow any formal changes, the functioning of the Community was undoubtedly modified in a way which partially satisfied the demands of General de Gaulle. On the one hand, in the event of a serious disagreement, France could still pursue a policy of the "empty chair" again, which would inevitably encourage its partners to seek conciliation. On the other hand, the Commission, from then on committed to a policy of prudence and caution, would, in practice, lose some of its freedom of action, particularly in the field of external relations, where its almost "governmental" style of behavior irritated the French government. Moreover, the crisis had increased the control of national governments over the Community, in accordance with French desires, since the modification concerning the balance of powers among the institutions had, in fact, worked out in favor of the Council of Ministers. This change enhanced the governmental nature of the system to the detriment of its supranational aspect.

Nevertheless, this evolution, favored by the French government, was not altogether advantageous of it, since it aroused the opposition of the Five, and especially of West Germany, to France's attempts to impose its point of view within the Common

Market. In response to this French offensive which had first tried to impose its point of view within the EEC and then, having failed, attacked the system itself, a German opposition emerged, based on a defense of the Community, although probably motivated more by tactics rather than by a community spirit.

Although French policy in the EEC, directed toward obtaining, without concessions, an agricultural financing regulation consistent with its interests, was relatively unsuccessful, the offensive the French government launched later against the Community organization itself proved to be more advantageous, since it achieved its technical and economic aims, while the institutional setback was tempered by a considerable victory on the political level.

The crisis, "sooner or later inevitable," according to General de Gaulle, had been caused in the first place by the supranational nature of the proposals put forward and defended by the Commission. Since it was, therefore, a party to the conflict and, as such, formally disclaimed by France, the Commission was unable to play a major role in the settlement of the crisis. The fact that the Council of Ministers alone was responsible for finding a solution to the conflict has, to a certain extent, given the impression that the Common Market is the framework and cause of "a persistent example of traditional interstate politics."[21]

The 1965 crisis inevitably raises certain questions concerning the specificity of the EEC as an international organization and the role which, by virtue of its special institutions, it is in a position to play in the relations among its members.

Doesn't the very existence of the crisis validate the argument according to which "economic and social decisions tend to spill over into the political area"?[22] Doesn't it prove that the enmeshment functioned too well and that General de Gaulle "feared the dynamism of the system and the fact that the Commission was so successful in maximizing the spillover process and in establishing itself as a political authority?"[23] The French attacks contributed, in fact, to the emergence of the original role of the Commission —whose powers exceed those of a general secretariat of a classical international organization—and the propensity of the community system to restrict the freedom of action of its members due to the integration process to which they are committed.

But although the development of the crisis validates, up to a point, and in some ways negatively, the spillover theories, its outcome, on the other hand, shows its limitations.

This is doubtless why the authors who hold these theories—especially E. Haas—have amended their initial propositions and have come to the conclusion, as has Leon Lindberg, that "the integrationist process is discontinuous, subject to the intervention of *Grosspolitik*, and the spillover process depends as much on political options as on economic dynamism."[24]

This revision, while taking into account the "lessons learned from General de Gaulle," also confirms the analyses carried out earlier by Aron and Hoffmann which, to a certain extent, have been confirmed *a posteriori* by the 1965 crisis. These analyses pointed out, in fact, that a crisis may arise within the community framework when it concerns problems extending beyond the field of welfare only and entering the area of "high politics": "When grandeur and prestige, rank and security, domination and dependence are at stake, we are fully within the realm of traditional interstate politics. There are no actors, no constituents other than governments. . . . It has been said that supranational bodies like the Common Market Commission make possible among nations the elaboration of majority decisions with objectivity . . . for it provides and pressures the separate nations' representatives with proposals that take only the common interest into account. The trouble is that in the range of higher politics, such objectivity becomes almost impossible."[25]

Since the Commission's proposals concerning agricultural policy had important political implications and foreshadowed what might occur in other areas, they were undoubtedly connected with "high politics." The role played by the Commission in the first, and to a certain extent technical, phase of the conflict and, in contrast, its lack of a role in the second phase and outcome of the crisis defines fairly precisely the limitations of its action. On the other hand, the Council of Ministers seems to have acted, under the circumstances, not so much as a Community body as an intergovernmental organization, within which, in the classical manner, the members confronted each other.

The Community system has shown itself to be, not so much a means of limiting the exercise of power by its members, but the framework and even the stake of these demonstrations.

The 1965 crisis can be interpreted differently according to whether the emphasis is placed on the dependence of the member countries on the community system or on the way it is used to achieve national aims. But in any case, it has shown that the Common Market is dependent on a political environment over which, in the final analysis, it has little control.

Notes:

[1] For a detailed account of these problems, cf. especially, John Newhouse, *30 Juin 1965 Crise à Bruxelles*, Paris Fondation nationale des sciences politiques, 1968, Miriam Camps, *European Unification in the Sixties. From the Veto to the Crisis*, London, O.U.P., 1967.

[2] J. Newhouse, *op. cit.*, p. 26.

[3] Leon Lindberg, "Integration as a Source of Stress on the European Community System," *International Organization* (2), 1966, pp. 233–63.

[4] *Le Monde*, July 2, 1965.

[5] *8e Rapport général sur l'activité de la Communauté* (*April 1, 1965–March 31, 1965*), pp. 248–51, 373–78. Cf. also J. R. Verges, "L'élaboration du système de financement de la politique agricole commune" in P. Gerbet, D. Pépy, (eds.), *La décision dans les Communautés européennes*, Brussels, Presses Universitaires de Bruxelles, 1969, pp. 297–320.

[6] M. Camps, *op. cit.*, p. 53.

[7] J. Newhouse, *op. cit.*, p. 101.

[8] *Le Monde*, July 3, 1965.

[9] France carried out this decision, in fact, by abstaining from taking part in the meeting of the ECSC Council of Ministers on July 13 and the meeting of finance ministers at Stresa on July 19–20.

[10] *Le Monde*, July 29, 1965.

[11] On the real scope of this extension of the majority vote to the EEC Council of Ministers, cf. A. Jaumin-Ponsar, *La capacité décisionnelle du système communautaire européen. Essai d'interprétation d'une crise*, Louvain, Vander, 1970, pp. 97–99.

[12] Press Conference, September 9, 1965. *L'Année politique, 1965*, pp. 436ff.

[13] M. Camps, *op. cit.*, p. 117.

[14] *Le Monde*, October 22, 1965.

[15] J. Newhouse, *op. cit.*, p. 145.

[16] *Ibid.*, pp. 154–57.

[17] *Le Monde*, January 19, 1966.

[18] The text in respect to the "procedure for majority voting" stipulates the following:

1. When, in the event of decisions to be taken by majority vote on a proposal of the Commission, issues very important to one or more member countries are at stake, the members of the Council will try, within a reasonable time, to reach solutions which can be adopted by all members of the Council, while respecting their mutual interests, and those of the Community, in accordance with Article 2 of the Treaty.

2. With respect to the preceding paragraph, the French delegation considers that, when very important interests are at stake, the discussion must be continued until unanimous agreement is reached.

3. The six delegations note that there is a divergence of views on what should be done in the event of a failure to reach complete agreement. The six delegations consider, nevertheless, that this divergence of views would not prevent the Commission from resuming its work in accordance with the normal procedure.

19 *La Nation*, September 14, 1965.

20 Gaudet, Michel, "La fusion des Communautés européennes au lendemain des accords de Luxembourg," *Colloque de Liège*, April 1966. Quoted by A. Jaumin-Ponsar, *op. cit.*, p. 141.

21 S. Hoffmann, "Discord in Community: the North Atlantic Area as a Partial International System," *International Organization*, (2), 1963, p. 529.

22 E. Haas, "Technocracy, Pluralism and the New Europe," in S. Graubard, (ed.), *A New Europe?* Boston, Houghton Mifflin Co., 1964, p. 56.

23 L. Lindberg, *art. cit.*, p. 32.

24 *Ibid*, p. 49.

25 S. Hoffmann, *art. cit.*, p. 531.

7

THE UTILITY OF THE EEC EXPERIENCE FOR EASTERN EUROPE
BY WERNER FELD

Until the late 1960s, the Soviet Union and the Communist states of Eastern Europe maintained an attitude of hostility toward the European Community. Its success, however, led the Communist leaders to attempt to revitalize their own "common market," the Council for Mutual Economic Assistance (Comecon) which had been operating with little achievement since 1949. Werner Feld describes the lessons that Comecon could draw from the economic integration of Western Europe, thereby throwing light on the effect on the integration movement of the political framework within which it must operate. This chapter originally appeared as an article, "The Utility of the EEC Experience for Eastern Europe," Journal of Common Market Studies, *8:3 (March 1970), pp. 236–71. It is reprinted here by permission of the publisher.*

The establishment and operation of the European Economic Community have evoked three major reactions in the rest of the world: admiration for the successful process of economic integration, displeasure over the actual and potential harm to the economies of the non-member countries, and a mixture of envy and apprehension about the increased prestige and power—economic as well as political—that has accrued to the member states of the EEC. These reactions, in turn, have prompted a variety of behaviour by the non-member states. Some were anxious to climb on the "bandwagon" of economic benefits by seeking to join the Common Market and applied for either full membership or associate status. Others attempted to emulate the success of the Common Market and, at the same time, reduce its harmful effects by establishing either customs unions or free trade areas of their own. The non-European developed capitalist countries sought to exploit the rapidly rising economic levels in the Common Market through multilateral tariff-cutting ventures, through which they hoped the internal Common Market preferences would be reduced and international trade expanded. Examples are the Dillon and Kennedy rounds which have contributed to the remarkable rise in trade between these countries and the EEC.[1]

In the East European Communist countries all three of these reactions could be observed. After at first playing down the prospects of the Common Market and declaring it to be doomed to failure, the Soviet and other Communist leaders a few years later paid grudging respect to the economic integration process as carried out by the "capitalists" in Western Europe. In the *Seventeen Theses Regarding the Common Market*, published in 1957 by the authoritative Moscow Institute of World Economics and International Relations, the Common Market was seen as a new method of dividing the capitalist work market, bound to lead to serious frictions and conflicts within capitalist society. It was doubted that the steps envisaged by the EEC Treaty could ever be accomplished.[2] But, in 1962, thirty-two new theses published by the same institute under the title *Concerning Imperialist "Integration" in Western Europe (The Common Market)* set a different tone. They recognized that the Common Market had stimulated production on a greater scale than anticipated and resulted "in certain increases of wages for the laboring class"[3] A short time prior to the publication of the latest theses, the director of the Institute had already stated in an article in *Pravda* that "in the Common Market one can observe a real technical and scientific revolution which carries with it a powerful regeneration of the industrial structure of capitalism. . . . The EEC has a remarkable vitality and has created objective situations whose elimination will not be possible without grave consequences."[4]

The East European Communist leaders were also apprehensive about the effects of the Common Market on their exports to the member countries and feared that a future common commercial policy of the EEC could be extremely disruptive to this trade. For these reasons, the Soviet Union demanded after the establishment of the Common Market that she and the other East European Communist countries be accorded the same preferences under the most-favored-nation clause which the EEC countries had granted each other under the Treaty. (Since under the GATT rules customs unions preferences are exempted from the application of this clause, this demand was refused.)

Another concern of the East European Communists lay in the field of strategy and high politics. They feared that the successful conclusion of the customs and economic union as set forth in the Treaty of Rome might lead to a politically unified Western Europe that would upset the strategic status quo; moreover, a united Europe closely allied to the United States would materially alter the world balance of power. And even if these events were not to materialize immediately, the prestige accruing to the Common Market through a successful integration process could have a psychological impact on the people in the East European states that would be detrimental to the interests of the Communist leadership.

Apprehension over the harmful effects of the Common Market on East European trade with Western Europe and over the consequences of successful economic integration in the EEC were key factors prompting changes in the organization of Comecon. Gomulka is supposed to have proposed personally to Khrushchev in 1957 that Comecon be developed as the answer to the EEC.[5] At the same time, the Czechoslovak and Hungarian governments also advocated that the East should oppose integration with integration. In 1962 Khrushchev expressed the view that, in response to the evolution of the Common Market, Comecon should establish a unified planning organ, empowered to elaborate common plans and to decide organizational matters.[6] Although the Rumanians refused to accept anything resembling supranational[7] decision-making, the Comecon charter of 1960, setting up a comprehensive institutional structure which had been lacking so far, as well as the Basic Principles and charter amendments adopted in 1962,[8] was a definitive move in the direction of the objectives set by Khrushchev and other East European leaders.

In the meantime, the East European governments made strong efforts to increase their exports to the Common Market, which were matched during the last few years by a growing drive on the part of Common Market firms to expand their own sales to East Europe. As a consequence, mutual trade in the period from 1958 to 1967 tripled. However, for the EEC as a unit this trade was relatively insignificant, representing, in 1967, only about 6 per cent of its total external commerce. On the other hand for the East European countries their trade with the EEC was important and, disregarding trade within Comecon, ranged from a low of about 20 per cent of external trade for the Soviet Union to more than 50 per cent for Rumania.[9]

The East European endeavors to increase trade with the EEC were motivated not only by the natural desire to find markets for their agricultural products and certain raw materials, especially petroleum, but also by their interest in obtaining certain capital goods with long-range Western credits and in sharing in the special technological knowledge of the Western industries. The pursuit of these objectives and the perceived need to neutralize the magnetism of the Common Market are likely reasons why the Soviet Union has in recent years advocated all-European economic co-operation, perhaps in the form of a free trade area which would safeguard the sovereignty of all participating states. In this connection a statement made by Chairman Kosygin during a news conference in London early in 1967 is noteworthy. Asked whether British membership in the Common Market would be good or bad for European development and security, he replied: "The very name Common Market is a drawback in that it is not 'common' because not all countries are free to join. Markets of this kind should be open to co-operation of all nations of Europe on an equal footing."[10]

In view of these Soviet objectives and the fascination which the integration process in the Common Market holds for many East European leaders, academicians, and perhaps even a segment of the public at large, one may pose several questions. Are the experiences of the Common Market during the last ten years relevant for the integrative efforts in Eastern Europe and can they serve as catalysts for further progress in that direction, either within the framework of Comecon or for a subregional group of countries that would exclude the Soviet Union? Would a transplantation and utilization of these experiences contribute to the eventual bridging of the gap between West and East Europe? Would such developments enhance the transformation of the economic and political systems of the People's Democracies towards a limited acceptance of market forces and pluralism which appears to have started to varying degrees in several of the Communist countries of Eastern Europe? In the following pages these questions will be examined and an attempt will be made to produce tentative conclusions and forecasts. But first two comments are necessary about the concepts to be used and the scope of this paper.

Firstly, no claim is made that economic or political integration is a value in itself. The purpose of this paper is simply to determine the utility of the experiences of one international system for the operation of another system, and if such utility is found to exist, an attempt is made to evaluate the potential effects of these experiences upon bridging the gap between the two halves of

Europe and on the transformation of the economic and political systems of the People's Democracies. While we will point out the necessary conditions for the application of the relevant EEC experiences in Eastern Europe and their possible consequences, it is to be clearly understood that we do not make any policy recommendations in this paper, especially as far as the use of the force of nationalism in Eastern Europe is concerned.

Secondly, although I am very skeptical that in the foreseeable future a subregional economic unit could emerge in Eastern Europe that would exclude the Soviet Union, there has been a great deal of speculation in recent years about such a possibility[11] and this is the reason that we have included such an eventuality in our discussions. Clearly, the trend towards the application of the profit principle, greater emphasis on the market forces, and increased decentralization of economic decision-making initiated by Yugoslavia, and followed to some degree by the attempted transformation of the economic systems particularly in Czechoslovakia and Hungary, provide a measure of plausibility for these speculations. But would the Soviet Union agree to the development of a subregional economic group that might reduce her influence on Eastern Europe and weaken her strategic position? Although extremely doubtful, one cannot completely exclude such a development which perhaps could come about as a consequence of a general understanding between the United States and the Soviet Union in response to mounting nuclear pressures and proliferation, aggravated for the U.S.S.R. by the severity of the Sino-Soviet conflict.[12] However, the Soviet action in Czechoslovakia is not a hopeful sign in this direction.

The Relevance of Common Market Experiences

For the examination of the Common Market's experience it is useful to divide it into operational and institutional experience. Since we are concerned with utilitarian and catalytic values of this experience we will focus on those EEC activities and policies which have had a measure of success as judged by the objectives of the Treaty of Rome. However, failures can also be instructive and therefore we will discuss them when they may have a bearing on the prospects of East European integration.

OPERATIONAL EXPERIENCE
The Realization of the Customs Union

Foremost among the accomplishments of the EEC stands the realization of the customs union through the complete elimination of internal tariffs and the establishment of the common external tariff, well ahead of the schedule set by the Treaty. A concomitant accomplishment is the progress made with respect to the free movement of persons and capital within the Common Market, although here the full objectives of the Treaty have not been reached as yet.

For Comecon the realization of the customs union is not a relevant experience and is not susceptible to transplantation at present. Under the capitalistic system the elimination of internal tariff barriers means that business enterprises can make their production, marketing, and investment decisions in such a manner as to be able to benefit from the economies of scale, and that resource allocation within the customs union is likely to be made in due time according to the principle of comparative advantage. On the other hand, even if the frontiers of the states within Comecon were eliminated, the distribution of output and sales and the allocation of resources within the area as a whole would still not be subject to the interplay of market forces, as in the West, but would have to conform mainly to over-all planning directives laid down by the responsible authorities.

The use of tariffs with the outside world also has little significance except for bargaining purposes in the negotiation of commercial agreements. The primary controls on foreign trade are direct quantitative controls that regulate the flow of imports and exports in accordance with the requirements of Comecon and national plans of the member countries. Moreover, the formation of prices, so far at least, has in most cases been based neither on cost nor followed the laws of demand and supply but decided by government decree in conformity with the requirements of planned management. The internal prices of all Communist countries are separated effectively from the external ones by the institution of the foreign trade monopoly, and the instrument of pricing is used to provide preferences for goods produced in the member states for intra-Comecon trade.[13] Of course, this system also means that granting most-favored-nation treatment to third countries is nothing but a meaningless gesture since it is price formation and not tariffs that determine the preferential treatment of trade within Comecon. This also shows that in practice the Comecon area possesses the same protective armoury as does a customs union through the application of Article XXIV of GATT.

In considering the establishment of a conventional customs union or free trade area for a subregional grouping of several or all of the People's Democracies, one must take into account their differing levels of economic development. On the highest level we find the German Democratic Republic and Czechoslovakia, on the next lower level, Yugoslavia, Poland, and Hungary, and on the lowest level Bulgaria and Rumania, although the latter has made significant economic progress during the last few years and now approaches the middle-level countries.[14] The countries of the Common Market, on the other hand, had comparable levels of economic development when the Treaty of Rome was signed and this may have been one reason for its success. The Common Market authorities have always hesitated to consider the adhesion of European countries with lower economic levels and have in the case of Greece and Turkey resorted to the instrument of association which was to assist these countries in raising their level of development. If one were then to follow the experience of the EEC, subregional groupings should be concluded among countries of comparable development, although perhaps an arrangement between Czechoslovakia, Poland, and Hungary, as has been suggested,[15] may operate successfully.[16]

Of course, in order to draw optimum benefits from the realization of a customs union or a free trade area, the prices will have to conform to costs and the market forces must be given a measure of play. Clearly, if the prevailing trend in some of the People's Democracies is allowed to continue, one may expect the creation of economic conditions that would make elimination of internal tariff barriers useful. We should note here that the experiences with planning acquired after twenty years of Communist regime would not necessarily become a lost art under the new conditions. In fact, as the operation of customs unions and free trade areas in developing countries, i.e., LAFTA, the Central American Common Market, and the East African Economic Community, have demonstrated, a measure of careful intelligent guidance may be necessary to channel the play of the market forces in order to overcome the problems arising from differential development.[17] But what would be required for the successful implementation of a customs union or free trade area would be reduced emphasis upon the maxim of national sovereignty and economic egoism which at present characterize to varying degrees the attitudes of the governments of the People's Democracies. Since these attitudes reflect to a large extent the fears of most People's Democracies of Soviet encroachment upon their national affairs, one may assume that they would be much less pronounced in a subregional grouping that would exclude the U.S.S.R. In fact, it is conceivable that a regional spirit may emerge under these circumstances which would promote the meshing of national and regional plans with the accent upon the Community interest and enhance the understanding that short-range national disadvantages will be compensated in the future by long-term benefits for all members of the group. To ensure such a result, it would be essential to set up, as in the EEC Treaty, a definite schedule for the elimination of internal tariffs and for the establishment of a common external tariff, schedules which must be observed without fail.

If a customs union or free trade area were to materialize under the conditions described in the preceding paragraph, the prospects for a gradual transformation of the economic systems of the participating People's Democracies appear to be good, and this transformation, in turn, may also engender slow changes in their political systems. This does not mean that these countries would become full-fledged democracies of the Western type, but rather that they would follow the Yugoslav pattern under which the government seems to be moving toward offering limited political choices to the people and majority rule appears to become more and more established. Under these conditions, co-operation with the West would turn out to be more meaningful and beneficial than at present and the gap between the two halves of Europe could be slowly filled.

THE FREE MOVEMENT OF PERSONS AND CAPITAL

The Common Market's experience with the free movement of labor may in the future have utility for the East European countries, regardless of whether they are joined in Comecon or have developed subregional groupings. A large number of Italians as well as small numbers of other EEC nationalities have obtained work in member states other than their own: their social security rights have been safeguarded in ways similar to those of indigenous workers, and only few exceptional restrictions exist now against the free movement of labor.[18] Although the Basic Principles in Article I stress "efficient employment of labor," the free flow of workers from one Comecon country to the other is relatively small despite labor shortages that have occurred in East Germany and Czechoslovakia. Some Bulgarians have so far obtained work in the Soviet Union and a number of Hungarians in East Germany. There is also some movement of labor across the Czech-Polish border. Kaser sees indications of greater interest among some of the Comecon countries in expanded mobility of workers; if this is the case and if some of the East European leaders were able to overcome their mainly political as well as nationalistic objections to the principle of the free flow of labor within Comecon, the long-run benefits for economic integration may be substantial.[19]

The progress made by the Common Market towards the free movement of capital and full convertibility would also be advantageous to the East European countries despite the emphasis on planning in the socialist system. In fact, the Basic Principles in Article 7 stress that "multilateral co-ordination of plans and the resultant recommendations for specialization and co-operation should ensure that each socialist country has a balanced payments structure, notably through wider use of multilateral settlement. ..." However, only slow progress is made towards the latter goal in spite of the establishment in 1963 of the International Bank of Economic Co-operation in Moscow. This bank provides drawing rights for each Comecon member, which, however, must be settled before the end of each year. Only the rouble, but no other currency, is made convertible, and this convertibility extends only to Comecon countries, not to outsiders. In the meantime, the flow of capital is manipulated through cumbersome mutual exchange-rate adjustments or special capital lending operations.[20]

During the twenty-second meeting of the Comecon Council, Hungary, Poland, and Czechoslovakia pressed for greater currency convertibility, hoping that such a development would not only benefit intra-Comecon trade but also trade with third countries.[21] But no progress was made during this meeting or during the Comecon Summit Conference, held a few weeks later in Moscow in April 1969. The only tangible result of that conference was an agreement concluded among the Comecon members which stressed the necessity of setting up an investment bank in order to finance projects involving joint co-operation. However, it should be noted that this agreement did not actually establish such a bank, but merely emphasized the need for this action.[22]

The problem of convertibility would of course also plague any subregional arrangement. In fact, one of the most important objectives of the economic reforms in Czechoslovakia and Hungary had been to increase their holdings of convertible currency in order to purchase goods needed from the West. Intelligent planning of the subregional integration process and emphasis on the Community rather than the national interest by the participating countries may be useful in surmounting this obstacle eventually. The EEC countries have learned from bitter experience that common monetary policies are also needed for the proper functioning of the Common Market. This experience should be useful for the People's Democracies, and a common monetary unit would perhaps solve their convertibility woes better than any other device.

Increased mobility of labor within Eastern Europe may set into motion a gradual process of political socialization which could broaden the views of guest workers and the people in the host countries. If this were the case, one could argue that the expanded labor movement could have indirect, long-range beneficial effects for bridging the gap between East and West Europe. But so far sufficient studies on the social and political effects of border-crossing labor mobility are lacking that would offer empirical support for this argument. In fact, some of the experiences with South European labor in the northern EEC countries suggest the emergence of a certain hostility between guest workers and the indigenous population.

Equally uncertain is the effect of greater labor mobility on the transformation of the economic and political systems of the People's Democracies. It seems safest, therefore, to state that no special effect can be foreseen at this stage.

As far as increased mobility of capital is concerned, especially if it were based on a greater currency convertibility, the benefits for bridging the gap between East and West Europe are obvious; the effects on the transformation of the economic systems of the People's Democracies are not clear, but given the trend towards the greater play of the market forces and profit incentives, increased mobility of capital is likely to make a contribution to this transformation.

BORDER-CROSSING COLLABORATION

Some of the most important provisions of the Treaty of Rome deal with the preservation of free competition, a fundamental corollary to ensuring the free play of the market forces upon which the Common Market is based. While experience in this field *per se* is not relevant for the socialist economies of the People's Democracies or Comecon as a whole, the efforts of the EEC Commission to reconcile these provisions with the need for the creation of large, border-crossing enterprises and collaboration ventures that can fully exploit the economies of scale of the regional EEC market have a bearing on the development within Eastern Europe. The Commission has encouraged border-crossing collaboration between companies of different EEC countries in the fields of production, marketing, and research (as well as full mergers) because it feels that the interlacement of economic relations engendered by these co-operative ventures is likely to contribute to the process of integration.[23] Similar collaboration activities within Comecon would conform to the Basic Principles which stress in Article I the "rational distribution of the productive forces throughout the world socialist system, efficient employment of . . . material resources . . . [and] gradual removal of historical differences in the economic levels of the socialist countries." But although co-ordinated research on a Comecon-wide basis seems to have been agreed upon for various industrial branches, and plans towards country specialization based on optimal plant size or an area's comparative advantage are being made for some industries, border-crossing co-operation between plants of different countries has only been carried out to a minor degree.[24] An example is the collaboration between Czech and Polish tractor plants, which is an effort at joint production of one tractor model and also involves the co-ordination of planning and investments.[25] Czechoslovak industry, already over-diversified, would welcome additional collaboration agreements which would provide bigger production runs for their factories and could accelerate the rates of growth in the Comecon countries.[26] Further evidence of the Czechoslovak interest in border-crossing collaboration can be found in the organization of an international colloquium by the School of Advanced Economic Studies in Prague in April 1969 during which several Czech, Polish, and French participants delivered papers on the concentration of production within the framework of international economic integration. Reports from the Comecon Summit Conference held during the same month in Moscow also suggest an increased emphasis on the principle of collaboration between enterprises of different Comecon member states.[27] But whether in fact a higher degree of such collaboration will emerge in the future is uncertain because experience has shown that Comecon principles are not always translated into reality.

In addition to the relatively few instances of transnational collaboration between individual enterprises, there have also been other forms of international industrial co-operation in Eastern Europe. Oil and gas pipe lines have been used jointly by several Comecon countries and the national electric power systems have been interconnected through the establishment of a power grid.[28] But these activities have relatively low integrative value because they lack the element of interlacement (the German word *Verflechtung* is more expressive) among industrial enterprises of different nationalities for the purpose of production rationalization. Nor does the construction of a factory by one Comecon country in the territory of another have much integrative value because such activity lacks the continuity and mutuality of effort which produce the integrative effect.

Border-crossing collaboration would be especially significant in terms of integration if subregional groupings among the People's Democracies were formed, particularly if only a small number of countries were engaged in an affiliation. However, the same national industrial egoism that tends to impede the progress of collaboration agreements in the Common Market may be equally influential in the People's Democracies, and it will take intelligent guidance and persuasion to make the leaders of these countries see the common advantages to be gained from such joint ventures. Of course, the absence of the Soviet Union from subregional groupings may reduce the strength of nationalistic tendencies in these countries. On the other hand the ambitions of the leadership in some of the East European countries as well as ingrained nationalistic and conservative attitudes of the bureaucracy may militate against the collaboration ventures. Certainly, the experience of the Common Market has demonstrated again and again how difficult it is to find the common interest and to safeguard it against attacks from many quarters.

In terms of bridging the East–West European gap, border-crossing business collaboration is likely to make a definite contribution. The construction by Fiat of various factories in Eastern Europe constitutes both rationalization of automobile production among plants located in different Comecon countries as well as East–West collaboration of industry. In January 1969, Yugoslavia signed an agreement with France for greater industrial co-operation and the French Patronat has expressed great interest in developing collaboration between French and Yugoslav enterprises. Similar arrangements have been concluded between Rumania and France,[29] and other EEC countries, especially West Germany, have engaged in the same kind of initiative.

The future impact of transnational collaboration between enterprises of different East European countries upon the transformation of their economic and political systems is more difficult to determine. Such collaboration may well enhance trends towards decentralization, but it does not necessarily promote greater reliance upon market forces or profit as bases for production and price formation since joint ventures can be made to operate strictly in accordance with directives issued by intergovernmental planning agencies without regard to market forces and profit.

THE EEC COMMON AGRICULTURAL POLICY

One of the major accomplishments of the Common Market has been the creation of the Common Agricultural Policy (CAP), which has been hailed by most West Europeans as the necessary cement for the cohesion of the Community and the necessary pre-condition for the proper functioning of the Common Market.

While the CAP is fulfilling its major functions of Community preferences and increased farm income, the high market prices set by the Community organs have led to serious overproduction in certain commodities, especially wheat and butter. As a consequence, the cost for the support of the CAP has soared to about $4 billion annually. In order to correct these undesirable developments, the EEC Commission member responsible for agriculture, Vice-President Sicco Mansholt, advanced a number of proposals late in 1968. His plan was designed to ensure a standard of living for Community farmers comparable with that in urban areas; end the soaring cost of price support for surplus farm production; reduce the Community farm workers from 10 to 5 million, and turn over about 12.35 million acres of marginal land to other purposes, such as parks, green belts, or re-forestation programs.[30] The plan has aroused the vociferous opposition of some national farm interests, but not all. Nevertheless, it may well be adopted, in modified form in due time, as otherwise the cost of farm subsidies would continue to rise and assume astronomical figures.[31]

What relevance and possible utility do the CAP and the changes proposed by the Mansholt plan have for the People's Democracies? The Basic Principles declare in Article I that "the Socialists consider it their internationalist duty to direct their efforts to securing a high rate of development in . . . agriculture of each country commensurate with available potentialities, progressively equalizing economic development levels. . . ." In Article 3 one finds the following pertinent statement:

> The socialist countries differ in per capita farm land and in soil and climatic conditions: the exchange of farm produce between them will therefore continue and will increase. This makes it necessary to coordinate plans and explore possibilities for further specialization in

agricultural production in accordance with their needs and potentialities.

From these statements, which set forth objectives somewhat similar to those of Article 39 of the EEC Treaty, it is evident that the application of the EEC Agricultural Policy and of the later Mansholt plan would be useful for the People's Democracies, many of which continue to have economies strongly oriented towards agriculture. It would strengthen their national economies through farm rationalization measures and could improve their over-all agricultural situation through an increasing division of labor. The CAP as modified by the Mansholt plan is also congenial to the basic aim of Comecon, which is to attain regional self-sufficiency in temperate foodstuffs and consider net imports into the Comecon area as exceptional, although they are occasionally large in the event of bad harvests.

However, as Kaser points out, Comecon's agricultural program has been limited by policies of national self-sufficiency which have run counter to rationalization and cost-minimization measures.[32] While certain trade flows follow naturally from the differences in geography and climate, real division of labor has not so far been pressed nor have calculations of differential rent on a Comecon-wide basis been undertaken. This is understandable since the People's Democracies, especially Rumania, have been reluctant to play the necessary roles in any division of labor scheme. One important reason for this reluctance is the need of most of the People's Democracies to use a variety of agricultural commodities for exports to Western Europe in order to earn foreign currencies necessary to finance the import of consumer and especially capital goods without which industrialization and technical progress in their countries cannot make adequate progress. On the other hand, if a division of labor scheme were applied to agriculture, Rumania, Bulgaria, and the Soviet Union would be, for example, permanent wheat exporters, and Czechoslovakia, Hungary, Poland, and the DDR, wheat importers. We should note here that towards the end of the 1950s Comecon announced three major specialization decisions: (1) Hungary was to become a major supplier of rice; (2) Hungary and the Balkan countries were to specialize in labor-intensive agricultural output such as fruits, vegetables, and early potatoes; and (3) the Soviet Union was to supply land-intensive products such as wheat or meat whenever a member country's own production was insufficient.[33] However, a decision of the First Party Secretaries in 1960 made it clear that eventually each country was to supply its own needs. This last decision conformed to a strong desire of the Balkan countries not to be cast in the roles of agricultural suppliers for the other Comecon countries which may have reduced or eliminated their opportunities to advance their own industrialization schemes and increase their dependence on their neighbors, especially of course the Soviet Union. We should note, however, that the Comecon Agricultural Commission has synchronized research work for the member countries concerning the breeding of seeds and animals, animal and plant diseases, and weed killers. It has also worked on developing a uniform system of farm machinery through a program of comparative testing which reduced the number of such machines from 1000 to 400.[34]

Although political reasons may preclude the application of the Common Market's experience as an integrative device within Comecon, it could constitute a strong integrationist catalyst for a subregional group that excludes the Soviet Union. In particular, the rationalization measures proposed in the later Mansholt plan may reduce the number of farm workers and thereby provide the necessary labor force for the expanding industrialization of the subregional group. On the other hand, in terms of the long-range objective of eventually fusing the Eastern and Western half of Europe, the pursuit of a truly common agricultural policy by the People's Democracies with full division of labor might not be desirable since the implementation of this objective would then require a new shift of goals and expectations among the East European population. The same, of course, would also hold true for the Common Market farmers and agricultural policy. The effect of applying in Eastern Europe a farm policy similar to that of the CAP on the transformation of the economic and political systems in the People's Democracies depends on whether it is put in operation within Comecon or a subregional group. In the former case, it seems likely to impede such a transformation because it will tend to strengthen state control and enhance the hegemonial designs of the Soviet Union. Within a subregional group it may hasten the transformation process provided a measure of private ownership and of private incentive is maintained.

EEC EXTERNAL RELATIONS

In a true federation the formulation and execution of foreign policy is always entrusted to the central government. For this reason the determination of where control over foreign policy is vested also becomes crucial for evaluating the progress of political integration in a regional international organization which possesses supranational features. Assignment of foreign policy control to a central organ of an international organization would be one indication that the organization possesses a measure of supranationalism.

The EEC Treaty stipulates that the Community organs are not only authorized but in fact obliged to develop the principles of a common commercial policy towards third countries.[35] This obligation clearly imposes at least a limited responsibility of the Community organizations in certain sectors of foreign policy formulation. However, the elaboration of such a common commercial policy is making only slow progress and whatever has been accomplished so far does not apply to trade with the so-called state trading countries.[36] On the other hand, it is precisely the application of this policy which caused the Communist leaders so much concern because they feared that this policy would permit the Community to cut off simultaneously the trade of all six member states with Eastern Europe. This was undoubtedly one of the motivations for the non-recognition of the ECC as a legal unit on the part of the People's Democracies (with the very

recent exception of Yugoslavia, which has become intensely interested in negotiating a special trade agreement with the Common
Market.) In turn, this non-recognition was one of the factors
impeding the formulation of a common policy towards East
European Communist countries.[37] However, the most significant
cause for the delay in elaborating such a policy has been the wide
divergence in the foreign policy goals of the EEC member governments and their desire to use commercial policy arrangements as
instruments in the attainment of their general foreign policy
objectives. Another important factor has been the highly competitive struggle for East European business on the part of Common
Market industrial enterprises and the fact that a common EEC
policy may have rendered more difficult the procurement of large
orders.[38]

Although the Comecon Treaty of 1960 does not assign a special
responsibility for the development of common commercial policy
towards third countries to any major organ, one of the Standing
Commissions is concerned with foreign trade, but among the People's Democracies and with non-member countries. One of the
duties of this commission is to advise the Comecon countries on
trade with the West.[39] However, no general "common" policy
seems to exist to any extent, although some joint procedures for
dealing with third countries have been elaborated in bilateral
agreements or among individual enterprises. These agreements
are often not complied with and this may have been the reason
why, during the session of the Comecon Executive Committee in
Berlin in January 1969, new proposals were made for some sort of
common commercial policy towards third countries. For all practical purposes then the determination of trade policy towards the
outside world remains largely in the hands of the individual governments of the Comecon countries and is determined within the
context of their over-all economic plans. Thus, both the Common
Market and East European countries pursue essentially individual commercial policies. It is conceivable that if the Community
were able to develop a common commercial policy applicable to

the People's Democracies, they in turn might be compelled to move towards a uniform policy as well. Considering that the elaboration of a uniform external commercial policy undoubtedly has an integrationist effect on any regional organization, a common policy in the EEC, especially if it were to be perceived as potentially harmful by the People's Democracies, could through the formation of a similar policy by Comecon engender the strengthening of integrationist tendencies within East Europe. The same considerations would also apply to the reaction of subregional groupings in East Europe that excluded the Soviet Union.

Depending on the content of the commercial policies of the EEC and those of Comecon or of a subregional group, it is not inconceivable that they could be dysfunctional for the bridging of the gap beteen the two halves of Europe. However, given the basically favorable orientation of the Commission and the endeavors of the EEC countries, particularly France and West Germany and Italy, to improve relations with the East, such policies may tend to enhance the prospects for eventual success in filling this gap. The more congenial the respective policies, the better also are the chances that they will tend to promote the transformation of the economic and political systems of the People's Democracies. Peaceful engagement reflected in congenial policies of East and West is likely to weaken the grip of orthodox Communist leaders and increase the plausibility of slow liberal reforms, not only in the economic but also in the political sector.

In contrast to the lagging development of external commercial policy, the association policy of the Common Market as evolved over the last ten years has been quite successful, particularly as far as the relations with underdeveloped countries in Europe (Greece and Turkey) and in Africa were concerned. A survey of elites in the Common Market undertaken in 1965 has shown that the expanding circle of associated countries in Africa, especially those formerly under British rule, is a source of satisfaction identified with increased prestige for Western Europe.[40] In view of this mainly emotive response to the success of the EEC association policy one must attribute to it some catalytic value for integrative tendencies.

While the Comecon charter does not have any provision for an associate status of third countries, a special agreement was signed in 1964 by the Comecon Secretariat with Yugoslavia, making the country an affiliate member. Under this arrangement Yugoslavia participates in the activities of some, but not all, organs of Comecon and joins the work of many standing Commissions. In other organs she has observer status. This arrangement was a major concession to Yugoslavia and could be considered a form of association in the sense of the EEC Treaty. It is conceivable that a similar device could be used to link African countries to Comecon, in order to compete with the Common Market. So far, however, no formal effort in this direction seems to have been made, although Comecon organs seek to co-ordinate foreign aid activities to developing countries and differences in economic systems between the association partners might not present insurmountable obstacles to an affiliation agreement.[41] Another possibility would be the double association of a country with both Comecon and the EEC. It seems that Yugoslavia would be especially gratified if she were to obtain an association agreement with the Common Market. So far it is the Community, especially France, that balks at such an arrangement, but if the EEC member governments could be persuaded to follow a more creative policy for eventual union between East and West Europe, such a double affiliation may have all sorts of possibilities for the future. One could even go a step further and encourage EEC associations with some of the People's Democracies, now full members of Comecon. Association with Czechoslovakia seems to be out of the question for the present and the Soviet invasion of that country appears to forecast great difficulties for other Comecon countries as well. Nevertheless, Rumania, Hungary, and perhaps Poland could be candidates in the future if an arrangement for a preferential EEC agreement could be worked out that is decidedly beneficial for these countries and that could also satisfy the interests of the

Soviet Union. A recent agreement for considerable expansion of trade between the Federal Republic of Germany and the DDR[42] may also foreshadow significant changes between the two Germanys which, especially after Ulbricht's demise, may have important long-range implications for a fusion of the two sides of Europe, with the DDR possibly acting as intermediary between Comecon and the West. The instrument of association could be used by the EEC as a means of improving the economic levels of the more underdeveloped People's Democracies in a manner similar to that with Greece and Turkey. This, in turn, would greatly facilitate close economic co-operation between East and West Europe in the years ahead and later their eventual union. Finally, favorable effects could be expected for the transformation of the economic and political systems in Eastern Europe.

INSTITUTIONAL EXPERIENCES
The Aspects of Supranationalism

The institutional framework of Comecon is weak. The Secretariat, an effective organ only since 1962, plays the role of providing the essentially administrative functions for the organization but has little resemblance to the Commission of the Common Market with its extensive executive and supervisory authority. The operational functions are carried out by the Executive Committee of Comecon, which is composed of the Deputy Chairmen of the Councils of Ministers of the member countries. The Committee meets much less often than the EEC Council of Ministers and has neither the power nor the scope for decision-making of the latter body. In 1962, when the organizational machinery of Comecon was upgraded, Khrushchev advocated even stronger institutions endowed with a measure of supranationalism. He suggested that when taking decisions the common interests of Comecon as a whole should be taken into consideration rather than the immediate benefits for the national economies. If planning decisions were to be made on the scale of Comecon as a whole, he conceded that some interventions might have to be made in the management of the national economies. To promote Comecon-wide specialization of production, he declared that "the Soviet Union is prepared to reduce its output of some kind of manufacture if it proves more expedient to produce them in another Comecon country."[43] Of course, these initiatives by Khrushchev may have been equally or perhaps even more motivated by Soviet interests than Comecon interests, but it nevertheless constitutes an acknowledgement of the need for supranationalism in the Communist organization.

It is well known that it was primarily Rumania which squashed all attempts to introduce a degree of supranationalism into Comecon by threatening to withdraw from the organization in such an event. Undoubtedly, fear of encroachment by the Soviet Union on her political independence was Rumania's main reason for this threat and there can be little question that the suspicions regarding Soviet intentions were well justified and that they are shared by some of the other People's Democracies. As a consequence, the emphasis on the national point of view and the strict adherence to the principles of sovereignty and unanimity in decision-making has persisted and much of the planning of Comecon activities continues to be carried out through bilateral and sometimes trilateral agreements among the countries involved.

It is interesting to note that during the Comecon Executive Committee meeting in Berlin in January 1969 and during the Comecon Summit Conference in Moscow in April 1969, the Soviet leaders made new efforts towards introducing the principle of supranationalism into Comecon and sought in particular to create a supranational planning organ. The Soviet efforts were supported by Poland and Bulgaria. Already prior to this conference, Gomulka had expressed himself in favor of creating a truly common market including progress towards political integration. East Germany, however, did not commit itself to such a far-reaching kind of integration; she confined her objectives to integration on the level of industries but shied away from any political integration.[44] Rumania, of course, again refused any kind of limitation upon her national sovereignty and Hungary, anxious to avoid a crisis within Comecon, took an intermediate position. The result of the conference was a defeat of the Russian efforts. The final communiqué stated that all participants agreed on the need to improve and deepen the form and methods of co-operation of their economies, but also confirmed that their mutual relations were based *inter alia* on "complete equality and respect of their sovereignty and national interests."[45] Thus, little change can be expected in the decision-making methods and institutions of Comecon in the foreseeable future, but the co-operation between the Comecon countries may well become more streamlined and effective in the years to come.[46]

If the People's Democracies were to engage in the establishment of subregional groupings for the purpose of economic integration, the EEC experiences in the institutional field should be valuable. Tendencies towards nationalism and industrial egoism would need to be de-emphasized as much as possible in order to give the central institutions, which must have at least limited supranational powers, an opportunity to operate effectively. With the U.S.S.R. outside such a group, apprehension over Soviet control should not be a source for nationalistic orientation; rather, what would be required is the strengthening of the subregional group vis-à-vis the Soviet Union and for this the foremost requirement would be maximum unity. Otherwise the finest objectives of an integration agreement will be jeopardized and the end result may be failure. Moreover, if the long-range goals of such an agreement should envisage political union, the institutions must be sufficiently strong and prestigious to provide a realistic assurance that the expectations of the people in the participating countries can be satisfied. Only under such conditions can the necessary shift of such expectations and loyalties take place, a shift which will also need the support of a strong political will on the part of the leaders of the countries involved in the integration venture.

The effect of a strong institutional framework with supranational features in Eastern Europe on the possibility of transforming the economic and political systems of People's Democracies is hard to evaluate. If the Comecon organs were to be endowed with supranational powers and decision-making were to be carried out on a qualified majority basis, Soviet influence would be strong and the chances for transformation probably small. In a subregional group, the potential for transformation may depend on the views of the supranational leadership and how well the technocrats could be made responsive to meeting the needs of the region as a whole. The attitudes of the governments participating in the integration venture would of course also be crucial.

Speculations regarding the prospects for bridging the East–West gap in Europe are equally hazardous. In order to succeed in the supranational experiment, the newly formed economic unit may adopt at first a policy of autarchy which would tend to impede any bridging efforts. But once such a unit had gained greater strength, close co-operation between East and West Europe might become very attractive. Much may also hinge on the attitudes of the Western countries and their genuine interest in helping the East European grouping obtain the benefits of West European integration experiences. Other influential factors may be the strength of an "all-European" ideology in Western Europe, the perceived advantages of Western economic assistance for Eastern Europe, and the urgency for greater co-operation between all advanced countries in order to meet the needs of the Third World.

CIVIL SERVICE

The civil service of the European Community, amounting to over 5,000 people, constitutes a potential force for the progress of economic and political integration. Many entered the service of the Community because they were convinced "Europeans" and saw in integration the wave of the future. Others, perhaps more materialistic, were attracted by the relatively high salaries during the first years of the European Coal and Steel Community and its two sister organizations, the EEC and Euratom. All of them believed that the better the integration process moved forward, the greater would be their rewards in terms of influence, prestige, and salaries.

The rise in nationalism and the adverse political conditions created by this development for the progress of economic and especially political integration have of course dampened the spirit of many Eurocrats and destroyed many of the hopes nourished earlier. The increasing importance assumed by the national bureaucracy of the member states in Community decision-making has further undermined the *esprit* of many Community officials and their morale is at a low ebb. According to a survey undertaken early in 1969 nearly 66 per cent of all Community civil servants are ready to give up their positions for an approximately equivalent position elsewhere.[47] Nevertheless, while under the prevailing conditions (which may change in the future) the integrative effect of the EEC bureaucracy cannot but be very small indeed, it continues to operate in the daily interaction with the officials of the national governments and representatives of nongovernmental organizations. Moreover, the large amount of technical operations and decisions in which the Eurocrats are engaged touch a multitude of people in the Community and make them aware continuously of the work and existence of the Common Market and its objectives.

The number of civil servants in the Secretariat of Comecon is considerably smaller than that of the European Community. The authorized strength has been reported as 700, but, as Kaser reports, 200 positions were unfilled in 1964.[48] Moreover, the Secretariat also provides manpower for the various standing Commissions; on the other hand, the governments of the countries where the Commissions are located also furnish their own officials for these bodies. Kaser characterizes the Comecon Secretariat as "intergovernmental," which signifies that its officials are not to perceive their work in international or supranational terms as such notions are considered "unpalatable to their governments."[49] Of course, the philosophy of communism unites the staff members of the Secretariat with their governments, but this clearly can produce only limited integrative effects for a purely regional organization.[50]

If Comecon or any subregional grouping of the People's Democracies wanted to avail itself of the integrative value of an international civil service, it would need to stimulate the necessary international or supranational spirit in its officials. This could best be done by an explicit civil service statute that would stress this spirit by stating that once appointed they are no longer servants of the country of which they are citizens but servants of the regional organization, whatever its name might be. In addition, their duties and rights should be spelled out in detail and their new status must be respected by the member countries. Perhaps a stipulation should be included in the statute that would ensure equal access to the civil service by party and non-party members alike. Such a stipulation could eventually contribute to the transformation of the economic and political systems of the People's Democracies. On the other hand, the national bureaucracies must seek to de-emphasize their normally conservative attitudes towards new centers of power and thereby permit the integrative effect of a regional civil service to make itself felt.

PROSPECTS

In summarizing our admittedly highly speculative examination of the utility of the EEC experience for Eastern Europe, we can state the following impressions. First, the institution of an effective customs union in terms of the optimization of resource uses makes sense only if the price formation approximates as closely as possible the cost of goods produced in the member countries of Comecon or any subregional groupings that were formed in Eastern Europe. Second, full rationalization of industrial and agricultural investments, production, and marketing (which is one of the most significant potential benefits accruing from the establishment of a common market and the process of integration) requires the restraint of egocentric tendencies currently existing in the People's Democracies, although the political motivations for these tendencies are understandable and in fact may be most laudatory as far as the Comecon relationship is concerned. However, for a subregional grouping, excluding the Soviet Union, such tendencies would hardly be acceptable, as quests for self-sufficiency and the elaboration of a common regional interest are incompatible. Third, a measure of supranationalism and a viable international civil service are necessary to ensure definite progress of economic integration. Again, if nationalistic tendencies should persist in future subregional groupings, they would seriously impede the success of such groupings as far as economic and political integration are concerned.

What are the prospects that some of the obstacles to the utilization of the EEC experience in Eastern Europe could be surmounted? With respect to the formation of prices, the greatest obstacle, we have already noted the leadership of Yugoslavia in using cost and market forces for their determination—an approach which may in due time be emulated to varying degrees by some of the other People's Democracies. Koehler reports on the reforms of industrial prices in the DDR and states that these reforms were initiated in 1963 with the expectation that within five years prices would be based on prime costs of production, subsidies largely eliminated, and the differential treatment in pricing consumer and capital goods largely overcome.[51] Similar reforms had also been planned in Czechoslovakia and presumably Hungary and despite difficulties their implementation has been initiated. Although a long way may still have to be travelled towards achieving a completely rational price system, the trend seems to be clearly established. This trend may be reinforced by the industrial co-operation agreements that have been concluded by a number of West European governments with some of the

People's Democracies, which include in certain cases the granting of licenses and the construction of factories by Western enterprises. Initiatives by private firms in the EEC countries have supplemented the governmental efforts and have borne fruit particularly in Yugoslavia and Rumania.

Kaser contends that the trend towards decentralization apparent in most of the Comecon countries and the expertise of specialized departmental officials in the co-ordination of longer-range investment programs and short-run trade agreements might bring an optimal program within easier reach than by "grand decision of a supranational authority" provided the problems of the comparability of prices and costs can be successfully solved. He concludes that "the more initiative that is accorded to each enterprise, the more the Comecon framework will approach that of the Common Market. Symmetrically the further Comecon evolves as a Common Market, the greater the pressure to increase the autonomy of the enterprise."[52]

If the level of economic development in the People's Democracies were more or less even, then one could fully agree with Mr. Kaser's contention. However, as we have seen, this is not the case. Referring to the lessons learned from economic integration experiments in the developing countries, it appears that in a region with countries of differing development levels, guidance of the integration process by a supranational authority may be indeed essential and that therefore the full autonomy of enterprises may be a hazard. Of course, once a proper relationship among the member states in such a situation has been established by the supranational authority with the necessary safeguards for the economically weaker countries, enterprises can be permitted to operate as autonomously as possible within the limit set by the authority. Apart from these reservations, Mr. Kaser's thoughts are intriguing.

In an examination of interactions of regional subsystems, Kaser puts forth a number of hypotheses, one of which clearly has some application to the situation in Eastern Europe. This hypothesis states that regional subsystems in which a superpower participates interact in such a way as to foster the formation of advanced forms of comprehensive regional subsystems, excluding the superpower.[53] One of the major driving forces for this development is the desire to gain greater autonomy vis-à-vis the superpower. Seen from this perspective, the goals of the People's Democracies could be either the formation of one regional subsystem with a very high degree of integration or several of such subsystems, all of which would exclude the Soviet Union. We have already commented that the attitude of the Soviet Union towards such developments is highly questionable, but the continued opposition of the Czech people towards the Soviet occupation and the lasting adverse effects of the Soviet action on the people of some of the other People's Democracies may induce the former to agree reluctantly to the formation of some subregional groupings within Comecon, but not to the complete destruction of the latter.[54] Comecon may then continue to be a mechanism for economic co-operation between the Soviet Union and one or more subregional groupings of the People's Democracies, but no longer engage in efforts for intense integration. In this connection, another of Kaser's hypotheses may be pertinent to some degree. It states:

> Comprehensive regional subsystems weaken other regional subsystems. . . . if (a) they hurt the interests of members of other regional subsystems and if (b) they are reasonably strong and offer rewards for participation or access to the benefits of the comprehensive subsystem is an option reasonably open to individual members of the other subsystems.[55]

Clearly, these conditions characterize the relations between the EEC and the Comecon members. The Yugoslav attempts to negotiate a preferential trade agreement with the Common Market and the very modest Polish, Hungarian, Czech, and Rumanian initiatives towards the EEC during the last few years, more discreet and cautious, are apt to weaken Comecon, even if they suggest nothing more than vague possibilities in the future. The

Soviet Union, more and more apprehensive about the stagnation of Comecon, might consider this an additional inducement to accept the formation of a subregional grouping within Comecon if it were to perceive that such development might strengthen the cohesion of Eastern Europe and thereby bolster its strategic position.[56]

Of course, unless the People's Democracies make use of the positive experiences of the EEC and exploit the lessons to be learned from the failures of the Common Market, their efforts to form subregional groupings may not be much more than establishing intergovernmental relationships with little prospect of leading to advanced economic or later political integration. Yet, progress towards political union of the subsystem or subsystems is highly desirable in order to produce a counterweight against the Soviet Union and perhaps also to obtain a better bargaining position against the EEC, which in due time might include other West European states. It will then become evident whether the national industrial egoism displayed by the People's Democracies is merely a reflection of their struggle to be independent of Soviet control or whether it is steeped in an extensive nationalism that will insist on the prerogatives of sovereignty and on economic autarchy, regardless of the circumstances. If the latter should be the case, the results of the subregional groupings will be disappointing and the East European countries may well have forfeited the opportunity to catch up to the economic levels of their Western European brethren. Rather, they will continue to be dependent in every aspect on the Soviet Union and on the goodwill and enlightened self-interest of a more powerful Western Europe. And the prospects for bridging the gap between the Eastern and Western parts of Europe and for the transformation of their economic and political systems will be greatly reduced.

Notes:

1 Cf. Werner Feld, *The European Common Market and the World* (Englewood Cliffs, N.J., Prentice-Hall, Inc., 1967), pp. 89–112, and Office statistique des Communautés Européennes, *Foreign Trade*, No. 2 (1960), pp. 14–16.

2 Cf. Gerda Zellentin, *Die Kommunisten und die Eingung Europas* (Frankfurt-am-Main, Atheneum Verlag, 1964), pp. 73–74.

3 Translated in *Current Digest of the Soviet Press*, Vol. 14, No. 34, pp. 9–16.

4 Quoted in Zellentin, *op. cit.*, p. 76.

5 Michael Kaser, *Comecon* (London, Oxford University Press, 1965), pp. 75–76.

6 *Ibid.*, p. 93.

7 In this paper the term "supranational" is understood to signify a partial transfer of sovereign powers to central institutions of a regional organization and their ability to render binding decisions on member governments and individual residents in the member states.

8 Cf. Kaser, *op. cit.*, pp. 87, 190–95.

9 Statistisches Amt der Europäischen Gemeinschaften, *Foreign Trade*, No. 7 (1968), pp. 18, 20, and Feld *op. cit.*, p. 151. Inter-Comecon trade varies from 80.6 per cent of total export trade for Bulgaria to 59.9 per cent for Poland (1962); source: EP, *Sitzungsdokument 1965–66*, Document 75 (June 18, 1965); reporter: E. Achenbach, p. 4. This is a much higher percentage than that applying for intra-EEC trade compared with total export trade. The percentage figure here is only 38.4 per cent from 1958 to 1968; sources: Statistisches Amt der Europäischen Gemeinschaften, *Foreign Trade*, No. 6 (1969), p. 14.

10 *The Times* (London), Feb. 10, 1967, p. 11. See also Jerzy Lukazewski, "Western Integration and the People's Democracies," *Foreign Affairs* (Jan. 1968), pp. 377–87, and "La consolidation de la CEE, obstacle au rapprochement avec l'Europe de l'Est," *Les problèmes de l'Europe*, No. 40 (1968), pp. 32–52. Werner Feld, "National-International Linkage Theory: The East European Communist System and the ECC," *Journal of International Affairs*, Vol. XXIII, No. 1 (1968), p. 107, Marshall D. Shulman, "The Communist States and Western Integration," *Problems of Communism*, Vol. XII, No. 5 (Sept.–Oct. 1963), pp. 47–54, and Pierre Le Gall, "L'URSS et l'unification européenne," *Revue Française de Science Politique*, Vol. XVII, No. 1 (Feb. 1967), pp. 28–46.

11 See John Pinder, "EEC and Comecon," *Survey*, No. 58 (Jan. 1966), pp. 101–17, especially 117, as well as Karl Kaiser, "The Interaction of Regional Subsystems," *World Politics*, Vol. XXI (Oct. 1968), pp. 84–107, especially on pp. 99, 105, 106.

12 In such a settlement the Soviet Union may, however, insist on the retention of the so-called Brezhnev Doctrine, according to which the Soviet government can interfere in the affairs of the East European People's Democracies for the protection of "legitimate" Soviet interests.

[13] Cf. Kaser, *op. cit.*, pp. 143–44; Heinz Koehler, *Economic Integration in the Soviet Bloc* (New York, Praeger, 1965), pp. 160–61; and Zdenek Suda, *La division internationale socialiste du travail* (Leyden, A. W. Sijthoff, 1967), pp. 112–14.

[14] Cf. Suda, *op. cit.*, pp. 70, 71, 121.

[15] Cf. Istvan Agoston, *Le Marché Commun Communiste* (Genève, Librarie Droz, 1965), p. 275.

[16] See also the study of P. Wandycz entitled "Recent Traditions of the Quest for Unity; Attempted Polish-Czechoslovak and Yugoslav-Bulgarian Confederations 1940–1948" (mimeo).

[17] Cf. Sidney Dell, *A Latin American Common Market?* (London, Oxford University Press, 1960), *passim*, and Peter Robson, *Economic Integration in Africa* (London, Allen and Unwin, 1968), pp. 11–62.

[18] CEE—Commission, *La libre circulation de la main-d'oeuvre et les marchés du travail dans la CEE* (Feb. 1967); see also for Common Market labor mobility, Helen S. Feldstein, "A Study of Transaction and Political Integration: Transnational Labour Flow within the European Economic Community," *Journal of Common Market Studies*, Vol. VI, No. 1 (Sept. 1967), pp. 25–55, and Kenneth A. Dahlberg, "The EEC Commission and the Politics of the Free Movement of Labour," *Journal of Common Market Studies*, Vol. VI, No. 4 (June 1968), pp. 310–33.

[19] Kaser, *op. cit.*, pp. 165–66.

[20] Cf. Erich Klinkmueller, "Gemeinsamkeiten und Unterschiede der wirtschaftlichen Integration in West- und Ost-Europa," *Europa-Archiv*, Vol. 21, No. 16, pp. 577–86, especially pp. 581–83.

[21] *The Economist* (January 25, 1969), pp. 40–1.

[22] *Agence Europe, Bulletin*, April 29, 1969.

[23] Cf. *Journal Officiel*, July 22, 1968; see also *Agence Europe, Bulletin*, Jan. 13 and 16.

[24] Cf. Koehler, *op. cit.*, pp. 88–142.

[25] Cf. Suda, *op. cit.*, p. 56.

[26] See Kaser. *op. cit.*, p. 164. Collaboration agreements require authorization by respective governments similar to practice in EEC, when financial participations are involved.

[27] *Agence Europe, Bulletin*, May 20, 1969.

[28] Cf. George Kemeny, "Economic Integration in the Soviet Bloc," *Problems of Communism*, Vol. XIII, No. 5 (Sept.–Oct. 1964), pp. 10–15.

[29] *Le Monde*, Jan. 17, 22, 1969.

[30] *International Herald Tribune*, Dec. 11, 1968.

[31] *Le Monde*, Jan. 30, 1969.

[32] Kaser, *op. cit.*, pp. 166–67.

[33] Cf. Koehler, *op. cit.*, pp. 91, 92, 144.

[34] *Ibid.*

[35] Article 113 [Treaty of Rome].

[36] Cf. *Agence Europe, Bulletin*, Dec. 9, 1968, p. 4.

[37] Cf. Pinder, *op. cit.*, pp. 110–14. On Dec. 13, 1968, an official of the

Soviet Embassy had for the first time a formal contact with a member of the EEC Commission in order to protest against the discrimination against the "state-trading" countries of East Europe contained in the adoption of the first stages of a common commercial policy of the Common Market against third countries. This contact did not, however, signify a change of the Soviet non-recognition policy. We should also note informal contacts and agreements between the Commission and Hungary, Poland, and Czechoslovakia regarding agricultural imports, likely to be followed by similar activities with Rumania and the DDR. See *International Herald Tribune*, Jan. 29, 1969.

[38] Regarding trade between West and East Europe, see also Michael Fritz, "Möglichkeiten und Grenzen des Ost-West-Handels," *Europa Archiv* (July 25, 1966), pp. 509–18; and Rolf Sannwald, "Die Handelsbeziehungen zwischen der EWG und dem Ostblock," *Osteuropa Wirtschaft*, Vol. XII, No. 2 (June 1966), pp. 91–114.

[39] Cf. Koehler, *op. cit.*, p. 96.

[40] Cf. Feld, *op. cit.*, pp. 141, 142.

[41] See in this connection the interesting comments of Arnold Rivkin, *Africa and the European Common Market* (Denver, Col., University of Denver, 1966), pp. 53–54.

[42] *International Herald Tribune*, Dec. 7–8, 1968.

[43] Quoted by Kaser, *op. cit.*, p. 93; for additional details see pp. 91–100 and Suda, *op. cit.*, pp. 42–45.

[44] *Le Monde*, April 24, 26, 1969; see also *Le Monde*, Jan. 21, 1969, and *The Economist* (Jan. 25, 1969), pp. 40–41.

[45] *Agence Europe, Bulletin*, April 29, 1969.

[46] See *International Herald Tribune*, May 12, 1969.

[47] *Le Monde*, April 27–28, 1969.

[48] Kaser, *op. cit.*, p. 127.

[49] *Ibid.*, p. 169.

[50] Cf. Agoston, *op. cit.*, pp. 272–73. The views of Hacker and Uschakow, *Die Integration Ost Europas 1961 bis 1965* (Cologne, Verlag Wissenschaft und Politik 1965), expressed on p. 127 are questionable.

[51] Koehler, *op. cit.*, p. 190.

[52] Kaser, *op. cit.*, pp. 170–71.

[53] *Ibid.*, p. 105.

[54] A parallel case to such a system, but in an entirely different environment, may be the Andean Group within LAFTA—Bolivia, Chile, Colombia, Ecuador, Peru, Venezuela. This group was formed in 1966 in order to accelerate the process of integration among them. Another parallel case until July 1, 1968, was the Benelux system, within the EEC.

[55] *Ibid.*, p. 101.

[56] The Poles suggested greater integration as a means to tie the DDR to East Europe and neutralize the economic influences of West Germany. See *Le Monde*, Jan. 26, 27, 1969.

BIBLIOGRAPHY

The origins of the European "idea," or the concept of a united Europe, have been uncovered by Denis de Rougemont, *The Meaning of Europe* (London, 1965) and Federico Chabod, *Storia dell'idea d'Europa* (Bari, 1961), while a succinct summary is provided in the articles by Jean Baptiste Duroselle and Altiero Spinelli in C. Grove Haines, ed., *European Integration* (Baltimore, 1957), pp. 11–20 and 37–63. Pierre Renouvin traces the federal idea through the political thought of the nineteenth century in a lecture given at Oxford University, published as *L'Idée de fédération européenne dans la pensée politique du XIXe siècle* (Oxford, 1949). Hitler's claims to be the federator of the European nation-states are dismissed by Paul Kluke in "Nationalsozialistische Europaideologie," *Vierteljahrshefte für Zeitgeschichte*, July 1955, pp. 240–75. Walter Lipgen's extended study of federalism within the Resistance movements, *Europa-Föderationspläne der Widerstandsbewegungen 1940–1945* (Munich, 1968), is an exhaustive survey. The Italian Resistance, which was especially fecund in federalist plans, is documented in Charles F. Delzell's *Mussolini's Enemies: The Anti-Fascist Resistance* (Princeton, 1961).

Several good surveys of the activity of the federalist groups in the immediate postwar period and of the first attempts to create federalist institutions include Ernst H. Van Der Beugel, *From Marshall Aid to Atlantic Partnership: European Integration as a Concern of American Foreign Policy* (New York, 1966); Richard Mayne, *The Community of Europe* (New York, 1962); and Arnold J. Zurcher, *The Struggle to Unite Europe, 1940–1958* (New York, 1958). A reasoned defense of the Council of Europe is provided by Charles Melchior de Molènes, *L'Europe de Strasbourg: Une première expérience de parlementarisme international* (Paris, 1971). Ernst Haas's neofunctionalist study of the European Coal and Steel Community, *The Uniting of Europe: Political, Social, and Economic Forces, 1950–1957* (Stanford, Calif., 1968) provides much basic information as well as stimulating theory. Monnet's role in formulating the plan is described in Pierre Gerbet, "La genèse du Plan Schuman: Des origines à la déclaration du 9 mai 1950," *Revue Française de Science Politique*, July–Sept. 1960, pp. 525–53. The reaction of one major pressure group is analyzed by Henry W. Ehrmann in "The French Trade Associations and the Ratification of the Schuman Plan," *World Politics*, July 1954, pp. 453–81. For the economic principles of the treaty see K. K. F. Zawadzki, "The Economics of the Schuman Plan," *Oxford Economic Papers* (New Series), Vol. V (June 1953), No. 2, pp. 157–89, and for the first economic results, J. E. Meade, H. H. Liesner, and S. J. Wells, *Case Studies in European Union: The Mechanics of Integration* (Oxford, 1962). All aspects of the struggle in France over the European Defense Community are examined in the articles collected by Raymond Aron and Daniel Lerner, *France Defeats E.D.C.* (New York, 1957). One of the Italian negotiators, Paolo Emilio Taviani, gives a view from the inside in "Breve storia del tentativo della CED," *Civitas* (May 1957), pp. 23–53.

The negotiation of the EEC treaty was deeply concerned with the theoretical discussion of the economic results of participation in a customs union. The recommendations of the economists can be gauged from several fundamental studies, including Bela Balassa, *The Theory of Economic Integration* (London, 1961); J. E. Meade, *The Theory of Customs Unions* (Leiden, 1956); Jacob Viner, *The Customs Union Issue* (New York, 1950); and Tibor Scitovsky, *Economic Theory and Western European Integration* (London, 1958). These pioneering studies should be followed up by such reappraisals as E. M. Truman, "The European Economic Community: Trade Creation and Trade Diversion," *Yale Economic Essays*, Vol. 9, No. 1, 1969. On the negotiations themselves, see Alfred Grosser, *La IVe République et sa politique extérieure* (Paris, 1961).

Among the vast introductory literature on the working of the European Communities, the following are especially recommended for their clarity and conciseness: J.-F. Deniau, *The Common Market* (London, 1967); Uwe Kitzinger, *The Politics and Economics of European Economic Integration: Britain, Europe, and the United States* (London, 1963); and Michael Curtis, *Western European Integration* (New York, 1965). The Commission of the European Communities summarizes the results achieved each year in the *General Reports on the Activity of the Communities*, while the Statistical Office publishes a *General Statistical Bulletin*; these two documents constitute the basic working papers for study of the Communities, although hundreds of position papers, memoranda, recommendations, and reports are published by the various directorates within the Communities and by the Information Service. *The Journal of Common Market Studies*, published in Oxford, is devoted to scholarly articles mainly by political scientists, economists, and historians, on the activity of the EEC, while work in progress is listed in European Community, Institute for University Study, *University Studies on European Integration* (Brussels, 1972).

French policy toward the EEC can be traced in Alfred Grosser's *The Foreign Policy of the Fifth Republic* (Boston, 1967) and in two of his articles, "General de Gaulle and the Foreign Policy of the Fifth Republic," *International Affairs*, April 1963, pp. 298–

313, and "France and Germany: Divergent Outlooks," *Foreign Affairs*, Oct. 1965, pp. 26–36. Franco-German rapprochement is seen as the key to harmony within the Common Market in F. Roy Willis, *France, Germany, and the New Europe, 1945–1967* (rev. ed., Stanford, Calif., 1968). Wolfram F. Hanrieder weighs the importance of European integration in the development of West German diplomacy in *West German Foreign Policy, 1949–1963* (Stanford, Calif., 1967). Italy's position within the European movement is described in F. Roy Willis, *Italy Chooses Europe* (New York, 1971). Britain's early approaches to EEC and the Gaullist rebuff are painstakingly documented in Miriam Camps, *Britain and the European Community, 1955–1963* (Princeton, 1964). In preparation for its successful application, the British government published a valuable study of the possible effects of membership entitled *Britain and the European Communities: An Economic Assessment; H.M.S.O., Cmnd.4289* (London, 1970).

Specialized studies of the various aspects of the Community's work abound. Altiero Spinelli, who himself later became a member of the Commission, described the tasks of the Brussels bureaucracy in *The Eurocrats: Conflict and Crisis in the European Community* (Baltimore, 1966). Leon Lindberg takes several case studies, including the negotiation of the Common Agricultural Policy, to demonstrate the process of Community formation in *The Political Dynamics of European Economic Integration* (Stanford, Calif., 1963) and he joins with Stuart A. Scheingold in assessing what has been achieved in *Europe's Would-Be Polity* (New York, 1970). As general background to the European agricultural problem, which dominates much of the EEC's activities, one might begin with Michael Tracy, *Agriculture in Western Europe: Crisis and Adaptation since 1880* (London, 1964), before turning to Gian Paolo Casadio, *Una politica agricola per l'Europa* (Bologna, 1967). The role of agriculture in the "empty chair" crisis of 1965–66 is weighed in relation to the constitutional issues raised by de Gaulle in John Lambert, "The Constitutional Crisis 1965–66," *Journal of Common Market Studies*, May 1966, pp. 195–228, and even more fully in John Newhouse, *Collision in Brussels: The Common Market Crisis of 30 June 1965* (New York, 1967).

Regional policy has been under study for more than a decade in the EEC, beginning with the Commission's publication *Documents de la conférence sur les économies régionales* (Brussels, 1963), continuing with the *Rapports de groupes d'experts sur la politique régionale dans la Communauté Economique Européenne* (Brussels, 1964), and culminating in the extremely important report recommending creation of a regional fund, *Report on the Regional Problems in the Enlarged Community* (Brussels, 1973). European experts contributed to the useful collection of studies collected by the U.S. Department of Commerce, Area Redevelopment Administration, *Area Redevelopment Policies in Britain and the Countries of the Common Market* (Washington, D.C., 1965). The contribution made by EEC to the solution of Europe's great disparities of income between regions requires analysis of the work of the European Investment Bank through its *Annual Reports*; the financial contributions of the European Agricultural Guidance and Guarantee Fund (FEOGA) are summarized in the Commission's annual reports; Ugo Munzi reports on the work of the European Social Fund in "The European Social Fund in the Development of the Mediterranean Regions of the EEC," *Journal of International Affairs*, 2 (1965).

On the establishment of Community law and the working of the European Court of Justice, see Stuart A. Scheingold, *The Rule of Law in European Integration* (New Haven, 1965); M. Lagrange, "The European Court of Justice and national courts," *The Common Market Law Review*, Vol. 8 (1971), pp. 313–24; and E. Wall, *Europe: Unification and Law* (Harmondsworth, 1969).

Interest groups within the Community are described by Dusan Sidjanski in "The European Pressure Groups," *Government and*

Opposition, April–July 1967, pp. 397–416, and again, with Jean Meynaud, in *L'Europe des affaires: Rôle et structure des groupes* (Paris, 1967). On the role of trade unions, see Colin Beever, *European Unity and the Trade Union Movements* (Leiden, 1960). For a case study of the activity of national pressure groups attempting to influence the government's decision to join, or not to join, the EEC, see Robert J. Lieber, "Interest Groups and Political Integration: British Entry into Europe," *The American Political Science Review*, March 1972, pp. 53–67, and his *British Politics and European Unity: Parties, Elites and Pressure Groups* (Berkeley, Calif., 1970).

The degree of integration achieved in Western Europe appears high when compared with Comecon, the East European common market, as seen in Andrzej Korbonski, "Theory and Practice of Regional Integration: The Case of Comecon," *International Organization* (Autumn, 1970), pp. 942–77, and in Michael Kaser, *Comecon: Integration Problems of the Planned Economies* (New York, 1965). But one can find a cautiously optimistic appraisal of the extent to which a genuine Community is being created in Western Europe in Carl J. Friedrich, *Europe: An Emergent Nation?* (New York, 1969) and in R. H. Beck, *et al.*, *The Changing Structure of Europe* (Minneapolis, 1970).

INDEX

Adenauer, Chancellor Konrad, 28, 43, 46, 47

Ad Hoc Assembly, xiii

Agriculture
in Treaty of Rome, 66
common policy for, 67–68, 72, 132–133, 169–170
and "empty chair" crisis, 141–142, 146–147, 149
East European, 157
and Comecon, 169–172

Alker, Hayward R., 93–94

Alsace, 26

Anglo-French union, proposed, 12, 24

Arab-Israeli war (1973), xvi

Aron, Raymond, 106, 150

Association agreements (EEC), 70–71, 161, 174, 175

Balance of payments
in customs unions, 52–53, 57, 62
British difficulties with, 63

in EEC, 66, 74–75, 78

Balassa, Bela, 51–54, 58, 102–103

Beck-Goerdeler group, 8

Belgium
and WEU, xi
and NATO, xi
and Council of Europe, xii
and ECSC, xii, 28
and EEC, xiii
and EDC, 46–47
and "empty chair" crisis, 138, 141, 145

Bidault, Premier Georges, 25

Bonnefous, Edouard, 21

Briand, Aristide, x

Brussels conference (1954), 47

Bureaucracy
national, 65, 97
in Comecon, 168, 176, 179–181
in EEC, 179–180

Camps, Miriam, 143

Canada, xi, 24

Capital, free movement of
  in EEC, 66, 72, 164–165
  in Comecon, 164–166
Cartel policy, 71–72
Catholic Church, ix, 43
Christian Democrats
  in Council of Europe, xi
  in France, 27, 42
Churchill, Prime Minister Winston
  S., 11, 12, 24
Clappier, Bernard, 23, 24
Coal industry
  in ECSC, 19–20, 69
  problems of, 22
  of France, 30–31
  of Germany, 31–32
Coalition-building, theory of, 118–
  119
Cold War, xi-xiii, xvi, 97, 104,
  154–157
Collaborators, with Nazis, 3, 5
College of Europe, Bruges, 38
Comecon (Council for Mutual Economic Assistance), xi
  and EEC, 154–155
  as customs union, 160–163
  and labor, 162–163
  transnational collaboration in,
  165–168
  and agriculture, 169–172
  and external relations, 172–176
  administration of, 176–181
Commission (EEC)
  powers of, 71, 133
  relations to Council of Ministers,
  115
  agricultural proposals of, 132,
  169
  seeks increased powers, 134–135,
  138
  opposed by French, 140–141,
  144

  powers curtailed, 146–148
Communist party, French, 42
Comparative advantage, theory of,
  60–61
Confederation
  Resistance concept of, 8
  American, 8–9
Consultative Assembly (Council of
  Europe), xi
Containment policy, 15
Council for Mutual Economic As-
  sistance. *See* Comecon
Council of Europe, xi-xii, 21, 24, 27
Council of Ministers (EEC)
  and Commission, 115, 134–135
  during "empty chair" crisis,
  134–136, 138–139
  French proposals on, 142–143
Couve de Murville, Maurice, 133–
  134, 136, 138–139, 143–144,
  146
Customs union, theory of, xiii-xiv,
  54–56, 160–163
Cybernetics, use in political theory,
  86
Czechoslovakia. *See* Comecon

Debré, Michel, 147
Decentralization, 6
Défense de la France, 7
Denmark, xvi
Deutsch, Karl W., xv-xvi, 86–93,
  112–113, 123 n, 124 n
Dien Bien Phu, 45
Disarmament, 88–89

Easton, David, 102, 113–114
Economic Cooperation Administra-
  tion, 16
Economies of scale, theory of, 58,
  60
ECSC (European Coal and Steel

Community)
founded, xii-xiii
need for, 21–23
organization of, 23–28
economics of, 29–35
achievements of, 69, 72
tax powers of, 72
See also High Authority (ECSC)
EDC (European Defense Community)
proposed, xiii
treaty instituting, 40
French suspicions of, 40–41
and German question, 41–42
and Catholic Church, 43
defeated, 43–47
EEC (European Economic Community)
founded, xiii
achievements of, xvi-xvii, 67–72
agricultural policy, xiv-xv, 67–68, 72, 169–172
and economic theory, 50–62
political goals of, 62–63
joint policies needed in, 75–78
and financing dispute, 132–134, 136–137
"empty chair" crisis, 134–136, 138–144
Luxembourg agreement, 144–148
and Comecon, 154–159
and East European trade, 157–158
external relations of, 172–176
bureaucracy in, 176–181
See also Commission (EEC); Council of Ministers (EEC); Social Fund (EEC)
Elite groups, theory of, xv, xvi, 85, 90–91, 110
Energy policy, 68–69

EPC (European Political Community), xiii
Erhard, Chancellor Ludwig, 65, 79, 135–136
Etzioni, Amitai, 107
Euratom (European Atomic Energy Community), xiii-xiv, 69, 145
European Agricultural Guidance and Guarantee Fund (FEOGA), 68
European Atomic Energy Community. *See* Euratom
European Coal and Steel Community. *See* ECSC
European Constitutional Assembly, 11, 15
European Court of Justice, 71
European Defense Community. *See* EDC
European Economic Community. *See* EEC
European Investment Bank, 66, 76
European Movement, 21, 39, 44–45
European Parliament
powers of, 134
and "empty chair" crisis, 135, 137, 138, 141
European Political Community. *See* EPC

Federal union
Resistance plans for, x
theory of, 52–53
Federalist movement, x-xi, xiii, 2–16 *passim*
Feedback, theory of, 119
Fontaine, François, 39–40
Forward-linkage model, 119–120, 129 n
France
and EDC, xiii, 38–46

Resistance in, 7, 9, 11, 15
and ECSC, 19–20, 29–35
and EEC, 67–68, 89–91, 132–134
and "empty chair" crisis, 134–141
and Luxembourg agreement, 141–149
and Eastern Europe, 168
Franc-Tireur, 6
Frenay, Henri, 15

Gascuel, Jacques, 24
Gasperi, Premier Alcide De, xiii, 43, 98
Gaulle, President Charles de, xiv, 16, 65, 68, 78, 104, 134–136, 141–143
Germany
Resistance in, x, 10
and Nazi conquests, 3–4
and ECSC, 20, 29–35
and EDC, 40–42
and EEC, 67–68
public opinion in, 89–91
and "empty chair" crisis, 135–138, 145–146
Goedhart, Heuven, 7
Gomulka, Wladislaw, 156–157, 177
Greece, 70, 161, 174, 176
Great Britain
and WEU, xi
and EEC, xvi-xvii, 58–59, 62–64
and EDC, 43, 46
and free trade area, 57–58

Haas, Ernst B., xvi, 96–102, 104–108, 150
Hallstein, Walter, 101
Herriot, Premier Edouard, 44
High Authority (ECSC)
proposed, 19

powers of, 28, 69, 72, 98–99
Hirsch, Etienne, 25
Hitler, Chancellor Adolf, x, 2, 11, 13, 189
Hoffmann, Stanley, 94, 103–104, 150
Hull, Cordell, 13
Hungary. *See* Comecon

Indochina war, 45, 46
Industry
and ECSC, 21–23, 29–35, 69
and EDC, 44
in customs union, 54–56
and free trade area, 57–62
and Treaty of Rome, 64–66
and EEC, 67, 69–70
and economic union, 73–74
Infant industry, theory of, 60
Inglehart, Ronald, 94–96
Integration, European
defined, ix, 50–54
theories of, xv
and Resistance writers, 2–16
of coal and steel, 19–35
of defense, 38–47
economics of, 54–62
political theorists and, 84–85
transactionalist views on, 86–96
neo-functionalist views on, 96–108
research on, 108–122
and Comecon, 154–185 *passim*
Integration, theory of
economic, xi, 50–62
in political science, xv-xvi
and customs unions, 54–56
and free trade areas, 57–62
social communications approach to, 86–96
functionalist view of, 96–108
new research concerning, 108–122

Interdependence, theory of, 107–108
International Bank of Economic Cooperation, Moscow, 164
Investment, in customs union, 59–60
Ireland, xvi, 60–61
Italy
and federalism, x
under Mussolini, 5
and Southern question, 60–61
and "empty chair" crisis, 139–141
and migration, 163

Jacquet, Gérard, 46

Kaiser, Karl, 85
Kaser, Michael, 163, 170, 183–184
Kennedy Round, 70, 80, 135, 147, 155
Khrushchev, Nikita, 157
Kogon, Eugen, x
Korean war, xii-xiii, 22
Kosygin, Aleksei, 158
Krause, Lawrence, 102
Kreisau group, 10
Krieger, Alfred, 50

Labor
free movement of, xiv, 77, 163–164
in ECSC, 31
in EEC, 75–76
See also Migration
League of Nations, 8, 9, 24, 44
Liberals, xi, 79
Lindberg, Leon N., 101–102, 113–122, 131–132
Lorraine, 26, 29, 30, 33–35
Lüthy, Herbert, 39
Luxembourg, 28, 141

Luxembourg agreement (1966), 131, 144–148, 152–153 n

Mansholt Plan, 132, 169
Marchal, André, 103–104
Marshall Plan, 16, 22
Mazzini, Giuseppe, x
Meade, James, 56, 63
Medium-Term Economic Policy (1967), 79
Mendès-France, Premier Pierre, 45–47
Messina Conference (1955), xiii
Migration
in EEC, xiv, 77, 163
in Comecon, 163–164
Mollet, Premier Guy, 21, 43
Molotov, Vyacheslav, 12–13, 46
Monetary union, xvii, 52, 77, 165
Monnet, Jean
and ECSC, xii, 24, 26, 101
career of, 24–25
Moscow Conference (1943), 13

Nationalism
origins, ix-x
Gaullist view of, xv
Resistance criticism of, 2–3, 9–10, 14
and fascism, 7
revival of, 104, 180
NATO (North Atlantic Treaty Organization), xi, 27, 145
Neo-functionalists, xv-xvi
See also Haas, Ernst B.
Netherlands
and WEU, xi
and NATO, xi
and Council of Europe, xii
and ECSC, xii, 28
and EEC, xiii, 135, 137
and oil crisis, xvi

Resistance in, 7–8, 10
and EDC, 46–47
North Atlantic Treaty Organization. *See* NATO
Nye, Joseph S., 106–108

Oil
crisis (1973), xvi
in Comecon, 167

Pétain, Marshal Philippe, 26
Peyrefitte, Alain, 136, 145
Philip, André, 21, 23
Pinay, Premier Antoine, 40
Pleven, Premier René, xii
Poland
Resistance in, 9–10
Communization of, xi
and Comecon, 161–162, 164, 166
Political union
proposals for, 135
Communist opposition to, 156
Pompidou, Premier Georges, 140
Prebisch, Raoul, 60
Puchala, Donald J., 93–94, 108–113

Rambouillet Conference (1965), 135
Regional underdevelopment, 60–61, 75–76
Relative acceptance index, 89–90, 93–94
Resistance, European
and nation-state, 2–3, 8–10
activity of, 4–6
federalism in, 10–11
and Cold War, 13–16
Resistenza, 7
Reuter, Paul, 24
Reynaud, Premier Paul, 21
Rome, Treaties of (1957), xiii,

53–54, 65–66, 70–71, 133–134, 144, 166
Roosevelt, President Franklin D., 13
Rossi, Ernesto, x
Ruhr basin, 30–35 *passim*
Rumania. *See* Comecon
Russia. *See* Union of Soviet Socialist Republics

Saar, 20, 30, 32
Saint-Pierre, Abbé de, ix-x
Sandys, Duncan, 27
Schroeder, Gerhard, 137, 146
Schuman, Robert
and ECSC, xii-xiii, 19–20, 25, 27–28
career of, 26–27
and EDC, 43, 48 n
Scitovsky, Tibor, 58–59, 62
Security community, theory of, 87
Social assimilation
measurement of, 92–93
theory of, 109–110
Social Fund (EEC), 66, 76
Socialists
in Council of Europe, xi
in Britain, xvii, 43
in France, 7, 21, 43–44
Spaak, Paul-Henri, 47, 98, 145
Spillover, theory of, xvi, 99–100, 119–120, 149
Spinelli, Altiero, x
Stalin, Marshal Joseph, 12–13
Steel industry
in ECSC, 19–20, 28
problems of, 21–22, 33–35
of France, 30–34
of Germany, 30–34
Sully, Duc de, ix
Summit conferences (EEC), xvi, xvii

Supranational union
ECSC as, xii, 20
functionalist theory of, 104–108
opposed by French, 143, 144
and Comecon, 177–179
Systems transformation model, 120

Tariffs
abolished in EEC, xiv, 65–66,
67, 133, 137, 160
in interwar years, 22
theory of, 55–56
and Kennedy Round, 70, 80, 135,
147, 155
in Comecon, 160–163
Taxation
in ECSC, 72
in EEC, 72, 134–135, 138
Teheran Conference (1943), 13–14
Third World
and EEC, 70–71
and regional unions, 106, 162,
188 n
Tinbergen, Jan, 53, 79
Totalitarianism
in interwar years, 3
in Nazi empire, 3–4
Resistance view of, 7
Trade
in coal and steel, 29–35
creation and diversion of, 54–56
in free trade area, 57–62
in agricultural goods, 133
East-West, 156
in Comecon, 160–161
Transaction flows, measurement of,
87–88, 93–94, 96, 112
Transactionalists, xv
See also Deutsch, Karl
Transnational political parties, xi
Transport policy (EEC), 66, 69

Turkey, 70, 161, 174, 176

Ulbricht, Walter, 176
Underdevelopment, in EEC, 60–61,
75–76, 163
Union of European Federalists, 15–
16
Union of Soviet Socialist Republics
wartime goals, 12–13, 155–157
and Cold War, 18 n
and EEC, 155–159
See also Comecon
United Europe Movement, 27
United States of America
and European federalism, 11,
22, 70, 80
postwar goals, 13–14
United States of Europe, x, 12, 15,
44
Uri, Pierre, 24–25, 80

Value-Added Tax (TVA), 72
Vatican, 43
Viner, Jacob, xiii, 55–56

Welfare, theory of, 50–51, 55, 64,
73, 150
WEU (Western European Union),
xi
World War II
Resistance in, x, 2–10
Nazi victories in, 2–3
and German problem, 19–20, 39

Yaoundé convention, 71
Yugoslavia
and Comecon, 159, 161, 175
innovations in, 163
relations to France, 168
and EEC, 173, 175